INTERNATIONAL & MULTIDISCIPLINARY PEDAGOGY

Discoveries, Innovations, Challenges & Successes

INTERNATIONAL & MULTIDISCIPLINARY PEDAGOGY

Discoveries, Innovations, Challenges & Successes

Michael A Radin

Rochester Institute of Technology, USA

World Scientific

NEW JERSEY • LONDON • SINGAPORE • BEIJING • SHANGHAI • HONG KONG • TAIPEI • CHENNAI • TOKYO

Published by

World Scientific Publishing Co. Pte. Ltd.
5 Toh Tuck Link, Singapore 596224
USA office: 27 Warren Street, Suite 401-402, Hackensack, NJ 07601
UK office: 57 Shelton Street, Covent Garden, London WC2H 9HE

Library of Congress Cataloging-in-Publication Data
Names: Radin, Michael A. (Michael Alexander), author.
Title: International & multidisciplinary pedagogy : discoveries, innovations,
　　challenges & successes / Michael A. Radin, Rochester Institute of Technology, USA.
Other titles: International and multidisciplinary pedagogy
Description: Singapore ; Hackensack, NJ : World Scientific, 2023. |
　　Includes bibliographical references and index.
Identifiers: LCCN 2022024374 | ISBN 9789811261077 (hardcover) |
　　ISBN 9789811262111 (paperback) | ISBN 9789811261084 (ebook) |
　　ISBN 9789811261091 (ebook other)
Subjects: LCSH: Comparative education. | International education. | Multicultural education.
Classification: LCC LB43 .R33 2023 | DDC 370.9--dc23/eng/20220701
LC record available at https://lccn.loc.gov/2022024374

British Library Cataloguing-in-Publication Data
A catalogue record for this book is available from the British Library.

Copyright © 2023 by World Scientific Publishing Co. Pte. Ltd.

All rights reserved. This book, or parts thereof, may not be reproduced in any form or by any means, electronic or mechanical, including photocopying, recording or any information storage and retrieval system now known or to be invented, without written permission from the publisher.

For photocopying of material in this volume, please pay a copying fee through the Copyright Clearance Center, Inc., 222 Rosewood Drive, Danvers, MA 01923, USA. In this case permission to photocopy is not required from the publisher.

For any available supplementary material, please visit
https://www.worldscientific.com/worldscibooks/10.1142/12987#t=suppl

Desk Editors: Jayanthi Muthuswamy/Nijia Liu

Typeset by Stallion Press
Email: enquiries@stallionpress.com

About the Author

Michael A Radin is an associate professor of mathematics at the Rochester Institute of Technology, USA. Michael is an international scholar and enjoys developing and teaching mathematics and multidisciplinary courses and seminars in different academic systems. Michael spent his spring 2009 sabbatical teaching at the Aegean University in Greece and his spring 2016 sabbatical teaching in Latvia. Michael gained vast international experiences teaching in Greece, Latvia, Ukraine, Poland and Russia. Recently Michael developed and taught a course on "Pattern Recognition" for high school students in Rezekne, Latvia and developed and taught "Introduction to Business Start-Ups" in Ukraine and Poland. Michael considers teaching as a hobby and his primary aim is to make mathematics accessible to students with different preparation levels and from different disciplines in the traditional face-to-face and online environments. Michael's goals are to make online, international and multidisciplinary education accessible and to inspire students to learn. In closing, Michael enjoys exploring new teaching innovations in the American and foreign educational systems and comparing the similarities and contrasts and keep expanding the international and multidisciplinary frontiers.

Acknowledgments

First, I would like to take the opportunity to give special thanks my editor Rochelle Kronzek Miller for her support, encouragement and guidance with this new textbook theme. Her rigorous feedback certainly led me in the new innovative expansions of my pedagogical horizons. Her vigilant observations and comments were very beneficial with the textbook's theme, structure, comparison of educational systems, comparison of students' preparation levels, comparison of teaching techniques domestically and internationally, providing concrete examples of successful practices and all the necessary details remitting the math courses and multidisciplinary courses.

Next, I would like to thank the reviewers for their meticulous remarks and suggestions while reviewing the book. Their vigilant comments were very beneficial and enhanced the book's themes and contents, transitions between topics and rendered practical experiences. Their prudent recommendations also directed me to additional topics that I included in the content.

I would like to thank my colleagues at the Rezekne Technical Academy High School in Rezekne, Latvia. Aivars Vilkaste (the school director), Vineta Pavlova (English teacher) and the students for their support with the first pilot mini-course on "Introduction to Recognition of Patterns and Deciphering of Patterns" that I conducted there in May 2019. Their supportive feedback led me to new valuable experiences and to new teaching innovations, practices and principles. This mini-course guided me to write a textbook on "Introduction to Recognition of Patterns and Deciphering of Patterns".

I would like to thank my colleagues Jelena Malahova and Elina Gaile–Sarkane from Riga Technical University Department of Engineering Economics and Management for their encouragement and support in the development of "Risk Management Seminar" and to welcoming me to new multidisciplinary research projects. In addition I would like to thank my colleague Lita Akmetina from Riga Technical University Doctoral School for her support with my seminar on "Developing International & Interdisciplinary Research Coalitions".

I would like to take the opportunity to thank my colleagues Irina Jackiva, Boriss Meshnevs, Dmitri Pavluk and Igors Graurs from the Transportation and Sakaru Institute in Riga, Latvia, for presenting me the opportunity to teach Discrete Mathematics for Electronic Engineering and for welcoming me to the international, cross-cultural and multidisciplinary teaching and learning environment.

I would also like to take the opportunity to thank rector Veronika Khudoley of Academician Yuriy Bugay International & Scientific Technical University in Kiev, Ukraine and vice-rector Stan Kukhtyk for their encouragement and support with the first pilot mini-course on "Introduction to Business Start-Ups". In addition, special thanks to Anna Wziatek-Stasko from Institute of Economics, Finance and Management at the Jagiellonian University in Krakow, Poland for her support with the first pilot mini-courses on "Introduction to Business Start-Ups" and "Writing a Welcoming Selling Story".

Furthermore, I would like to thank my RIT colleague Tamas Wiandt and Wanda Szpunar-Lojasiewic for providing me the unique details and their interpretations that helped me to compare the similarities and contrasts between the American, Polish and the Hungarian educational systems. I would like to thank my colleague Witold Kosmala from the Appalachian State University in North Carolina for sharing his knowledge about the Polish educational system.

I would like to pay special thank again to my Editor Rochelle Kronzek for her support with this textbook and all my previous textbooks that I wrote. Rochelle supported me with the design of numerous diagrams and with special names of diagrams such as "Sources of Academic Innovations as a Pyramid-Shaped Diagram". In closing, Rochelle said "This will be one of many books ahead".

Finally, I would like to thank my parents Alexander and Shulamith for encouraging me to write textbooks, for their support with the textbook's content and for persuading me to continue writing future textbooks.

Contents

About the Author   v

Acknowledgments   vii

Introduction   xiii

1. **International Frontiers**   1
   - 1.1 Sources of Academic Innovations 7
   - 1.2 Positive Learning Atmosphere 13
   - 1.3 Multidisciplinary Education 16
   - 1.4 Expansion of International Horizons 20
   - 1.5 Summary 24
   - 1.6 Further Thoughts 25

2. **Mathematics Teaching Strategies**   27
   - 2.1 Hands-on Teaching and Learning 28
     - 2.1.1 Repetitive-Style Practice Problems 31
     - 2.1.2 Extensions and Multiple Re-Submissions . . 33
     - 2.1.3 Posting Notes and Videos 33
   - 2.2 Use of Multiple Colors 34
   - 2.3 Prompt Feedback 37
   - 2.4 Flexibility to Students' Feedback 38
   - 2.5 Summary 39
   - 2.6 Further Thoughts 40

3. Expansion of International Horizons — 41
- 3.1 Comparing Educational Systems 42
- 3.2 Building International Collaborations 49
- 3.3 Promoting New Seminars and Courses 52
- 3.4 Available Resources 56
- 3.5 Summary 58
- 3.6 Further Thoughts 59

4. New Mathematical Horizons — 61
- 4.1 Workshop-Based Calculus at RIT 63
- 4.2 SAT Preparatory Course 65
- 4.3 Discrete Mathematics 66
- 4.4 Introduction to Difference Equations 67
- 4.5 Recognition and Deciphering of Patterns 68
- 4.6 International Math Olympiad 70
  - 4.6.1 Math Olympics in American Style 70
  - 4.6.2 Introduction to Math Olympics 71
  - 4.6.3 Results of International Math Olympiad . . 72
- 4.7 Summary 73
- 4.8 Further Thoughts 74

5. New Multidisciplinary Horizons — 75
- 5.1 Introduction to Photography 78
- 5.2 International Research Coalitions 80
- 5.3 Risk Management Seminar 82
- 5.4 Introduction to Business Start-Ups 83
- 5.5 Summary 84
- 5.6 Further Thoughts 85

6. Resources and Feedback — 87
- 6.1 Available Resources 88
  - 6.1.1 Primary Resources 89
  - 6.1.2 Secondary Resources 90
  - 6.1.3 Asking the Right Questions 92
- 6.2 Alternative Resources 94
- 6.3 Feedback 97
- 6.4 Limited Resources 100
- 6.5 Summary 102
- 6.6 Further Thoughts 103

7.	**Promotion of Ideas and Innovations**	**105**
	7.1 Evolving your Innovations 106	
	7.2 Revising your Innovations 112	
	7.3 Selling your Innovations 114	
	7.4 Summary 115	
	7.5 Further Thoughts 116	
8.	**Online Teaching and Learning**	**117**
	8.1 Successful Online Teaching Practices 120	
	8.1.1 Online Mathematics Teaching Practices . . . 120	
	8.1.2 Multidisciplinary Online Teaching Practices 123	
	8.2 Expected Learning Outcomes and Beyond 124	
	8.3 Advantages of Online Environment 126	
	8.3.1 Why Teach and Take Online Courses? . . . 127	
	8.3.2 Online Conferences 130	
	8.4 Summary 131	
	8.5 Further Thoughts 132	
9.	**Post Pandemic Environment**	**133**
	9.1 New Technologies and Applications 134	
	9.2 New International Frontiers 135	
	9.3 Summary 136	
	9.4 Further Thoughts 137	
10.	**Appendix**	**139**
	10.1 Developed Courses and Seminars 139	
	10.2 International Collaborations 139	
	10.3 International Workshops and Events 140	
	10.4 International Conferences 140

Bibliography   143

Index   147

Introduction

The book's primary objectives are to welcome you to the abundant and meaningful international and multidisciplinary education discovery journey. In fact, if you seek out international opportunities for yourselves afterward, it will become a personal and educational journey to new encounters, successes and challenges as you learn what works in one place but another. You will also grow from exposure to other cultures and their practices and I daresay, become better teachers in your local as well as on-line environments. Most every local classroom is multi-cultural as well. The students have different backgrounds and different ways of internalizing information meaningfully.

The book will provide practical examples how to design, promote and teach various courses and seminars abroad. I will provide examples that I experienced with a specific pedagogical idea that is successful in one system, however the same concept may face unexpected challenges or fail in another system. Most importantly, the book will focus on applying feedback as vital tools that will guide you to the designing, promoting and teaching mathematics and multidisciplinary courses and seminars. The book's most important goal is how to make international and multidisciplinary education accessible to everyone.

The book will compare several educational systems as well as their similarities and differences. These include different teaching and learning styles, students' preparation levels, and students' interests and value orientations. My goal is to inspire you to embark on your own innovative discovery journey, seek out multi-cultural and international teaching opportunities and to eventually design, promote and to teach your own future courses and seminars. The most important goal is to effectively reach, effectively communicate information and help students learn. As we will see, the methods may be different, depending upon the country. The book will share about my own international experiences and hopefully motivate your own international experiences. These experiences include sabbaticals, designing and teaching various seminars and courses, new research directions and participating in multidisciplinary conferences.

Your own international experiences can influence and direct you in the design of your own future course or seminar. It is most important to effectively reach, communicate information and help students accomplish the expected learning outcomes. This can then lead to new research projects, design and implementation of new teaching innovations and forming new collaborations within your home teaching environment. I will share about the new challenges and risks you may encounter along the way and how to handle them. This then directs you to the corresponding questions.

What available resources lead you to the design of a new course and seminar? Which traditional teaching methods work in a new educational system? Which methods must be modified in a new educational system? What new methods must you design in a new educational system? Why in one academic system specific innovations are successful but not necessarily in another? How do you interpret and analyze feedback from students and colleagues?

While traveling you can compare the similarities and differences of different high altitude alpine systems with white snowy summits such as the Colorado Rocky Mountains in North America and the

French Alps in Europe. The first photograph sketches the sharp pencil-shaped crests of the Colorado Rockies:

The second photograph traces the tranquil-shaped crests of the French Alps:

The immediate question to ask: Why are there such contrasting differences in their shapes? In comparison to the French Alps, the Colorado Rockies have higher altitudes, stretch from north to south instead stretching from east to west, and as the Rockies are a much longer alpine system than the Alps.

You can compare analogous coastal rocky formations along the Island of Crete in Greece and along the Adriatic Coast of Croatia. You will discover similar high coastal formations and yet find many contrasts such as semi-arid marine landscape in Crete in comparison to green marine landscape in Croatia. In addition, you will discover different tones of white marble rocks and ranges of the navy blue colors of the water.

You can compare educational systems analogous to differentiating alpine systems and marine landscapes. The American and the Australian educational systems share similar characteristics and render sharp contrasts. Both systems educate students in English and have twelve grades. Homework assignments is one of the contrasting differences between the two systems; students in the American educational system are assigned rigorous weekly homework assignments that provide hands-on practice while the Australian local schools ere actually doing away with homework requirements. Which K-12 system provides better education?

The Polish and American K-12 systems both teach foreign languages. American students begin to learn a foreign language starting in seventh grade. On the contrary, Polish students can begin to learn a foreign language starting in second grade. Moreover, Polish K-12 system has language schools where students can study in a foreign language.

I invite you to this unique hands-on international and multidisciplinary academic journey and invite you to build your own individualized learning path leading to new international and multidisciplinary discoveries. I will also provide end of chapter open-ended questions.

Michael A Radin

Chapter 1

International Frontiers

Why teach abroad? As an instructor, teaching abroad will provide you very unique and interesting educational journey experiences that will change your teaching styles and perspectives. In fact, your international journey (whether online or in person) will build lasting international relationships as well as provide you with personal cross-cultural comparisons between cultures and educational systems. You will quite naturally start to collate your native culture and educational system together with the new culture and educational system that you are encountering.

Analogously to comparing educational systems, you can compare similarities and difference in coastal rocky marine landscapes along the Aegean Sea in Greece and along the Black Sea in Turkey. The first photograph renders the Aegean white marble rocks along the Island of Samos in Greece.

Figure 1.1: Aegean white marble shores.

While the second photograph depicts the white marble rocks along the Black Sea coast of Turkey.

Figure 1.2: The Black Sea white marble shores.

Even though the Black Sea is a sub-system of the Aegean Sea, you can see that Figures 1.1 and 1.2 trace similar coastal formations but resemble different shades of white, green and blue. The Aegean Sea and the Black Sea marine landscapes are similar but do render quite contrasting differences.

Analogous to analyzing the similarities and differences between the Aegean Sea and the Black Sea marine landscapes in Figures 1.1 and 1.2, you can study the similarities and differences between the Latvian and American educational systems. After teaching Discrete Mathematics at the Rochester Institute of Technology (RIT) and at the Transportation and Sakaru Institute (TSI) in Riga, Latvia I discovered that Latvian and American students had similar preparation problems with basic arithmetic. On the other hand, American students were trained to handing in weekly homework assignments and hence found more alternative solutions to solving graph theory problems in comparison to Latvian students.

Studying and comparing educational systems is a very unique and interesting journey but at times can be quite challenging due to cultural differences and contrasts in educational systems. However, it is essential to consider cultural differences and contrasts in educational systems as new innovative pedagogical tools. What successful ideas and practices can you share? What schemes and customs can you adapt during your elongated journeys? By teaching abroad you expand and strengthen your horizons as it is beneficial to analyze and understand the differences between teaching and learning styles, students' preparation levels and other analogous cultural differences that can emerge.

On one hand, you gain valuable cultural experiences while living and teaching in a new country. On the contrary, you can encounter numerous unfamiliar challenges that arise along the way. What potential cultural barriers can emerge while teaching abroad? What essential adjustments must you consider and implement in order to overcome the cultural barriers and to successfully implement your pedagogical innovations? What new ideas and innovations arise during your cultural and academic journeys? As a mountaineer you are destined to reach this hefty snowy crest.

In order for you to reach this solemn white zenith, you must consider challenges such as strong wind gusts, low visibility due to snow storms and foggy conditions. Analogously, you will encounter challenges in your international journey while designing and teaching courses and seminars abroad. Your primary goal is to reach your destination by achieving the expected learning outcome and to exceed the expected learning outcome.

Akin to reaching the mighty zenith, in my "SAT Preparatory Course" that I taught for high school students at RIT, the expected learning outcome was for students to gain practice in solving problems correctly and efficiently. Most importantly, to solve problems correctly and efficiently within the given time limit, perform well on the real Scholastic Aptitude Test (SAT) exam and get accepted to their desired universities. Students could solve many of the problems but had difficulties in solving them swiftly and efficiently within the assigned time limit.

In my "Introduction to Recognition and Deciphering of Patterns" that I taught for high school students at Rezekne Technical Academy High School in Rezekne, Latvia, the expected learning outcome was for students to gain practice in recognizing various patterns in great depth and in formulating and proving theorems using the proof by induction method. Many students were exposed to similar problems but not in great depth and especially encountered challenges with open-ended problems that analyzed derivations and proofs.

University professors in the U.S. have opportunities to collaborate with international counterparts on research, conduct seminars, as well as to sometimes teach a course overseas during their summers, exchange programs and during their sabbaticals. They often do. Analogously, American students have opportunities to participate in summer exchange programs and to spend a semester or year abroad in a different country. These are opportunities to learn a new language, be exposed to a different culture and lifestyle, and to learn a new culture in a new academic system. Foreign students from other countries also have frequent opportunities to study in American universities, to learn English and to experience studying in the American educational system. Quite many American universities have signed agreements with universities in other countries and offer faculty members and students these cross-cultural and multi-disciplinary opportunities.

Whether as a student, post-doc or faculty member, it is essential for you to take advantage of these unique opportunities during an exchange program or a sabbatical. The first crucial step is to gain international experiences designing and teaching a new course in a different educational system. The second step is to widen your comfort zone, experiences and intuitions by designing and teaching a new multidisciplinary course or seminar in your own university. These experiences and process lead you to numerous new questions that naturally emerge.

Why be innovative and teach in a different academic system? Will my teaching methods work in a different educational system? What is the students' preparation level? What cultural barriers can arise and how do I handle them smoothly? What themes do I choose for my course or seminar? What resources are available and what resources do I need? Sometimes you design new themes and teaching techniques in our own educational system and then implement them in a foreign educational system. At other times, you design new themes and teaching strategies while living and teaching abroad. Figure 1.3 presents some of the themes that emerge in both educational systems.

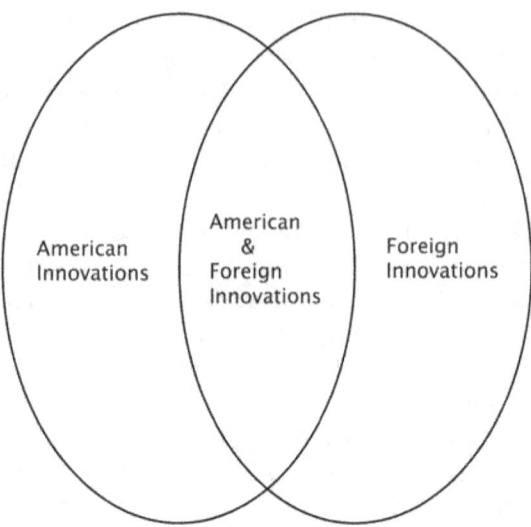

Figure 1.3: Innovations within academic systems-venn diagram.

For instance, My "Math Olympics in American Style" event is an overlapping region in Figure 1.3 as it originated as MATHBOWL event at RIT and then transitioned to a new event in Latvia. My SAT Preparatory Course that I taught regularly at RIT was only successful in the American system and appears in the American Innovations portion of Figure 1.3. My seminar on "Developing International and Interdisciplinary Research Coalitions" that I conducted at Riga Technical University and at EKA University of Applied Sciences in Riga, Latvia was only successful in the Latvian system and appears in the Foreign Innovations portion of Figure 1.3.

MATHBOWL and "Math Olympics in American Style" events were successful in both systems as the mathematics material is accessible to high school students. My SAT preparatory course was successful only in the American system as the SAT is the admission exam for American universities only. Few Latvian students were interested in studying in an American university for the bachelor's but instead wanted to pursue for the Master's and Ph.D. My seminar on "Developing International and Interdisciplinary Research Coalitions" was only successful in the Latvian system as Latvia is a small European country with international influences from its neighboring countries and from the European Union.

It is not uncommon that your colleagues can ask or suggest a new motif. The book will provide numerous practical examples of both scenarios as well as their overlaps resembled in Figure 1.3. My colleagues from Riga Technical University Department of Engineering Economics & Management suggested me to design and teach a "Risk Management" seminar. My colleague from Rezekne Technical University suggested me to design and teach a mathematics course for high school students. The upcoming section will focus on sources of academic innovations.

1.1 Sources of Academic Innovations

We define **Innovation** as an introduction to something new. We can also define Innovation as the tendency to generate new ideas and alternatives in solving specific problems. Innovation often requires thinking past the boundaries of your comfort zone. An innovation also expands the learning horizons and promotes new ideas and practices. An innovation welcomes open-ended thinking and welcomes leadership. A successful innovation should be flexible to questions and feedback and for future improvements. Innovation has been an essential problem solving tool for improvements and leading to further progress during the last 200 years (Radin & Riashchenko, 2017; Orlova & Radin, 2018).

Especially enormous technological innovations and pedagogical innovations have occurred during this time span as in no other time in the known history of man. Innovations have been essential trends in the new formations within the professional and pedagogical cultures. It is vital for teachers to introduce and include new activities inside and outside their classrooms. Furthermore, to develop and implement pedagogical innovations in the training and education and most important of all, to establish a positive hands-on teaching and learning environment for their students (Brown, 1958; Huberman, 1983; Venalainen, 2012).

The development of pedagogical innovations is therefore a pertinent tool for providing a positive and amiable teaching and learning atmosphere, positive feedback and for future improvements (Goodlad, 1967; Shields, 2003; Venalainen, 2012). Furthermore, according to the leading educational concept (Hunkins & Ornstein, 1989;

Spendlove, 2007; Von Glaserfeld, 1989) pedagogical innovations enhance teachers' emotional intelligence and offer a more flexible teaching and learning atmosphere. In fact, it enhances alternative teaching approaches and applying them to help students grasp and learn challenging concepts easier. These principles then direct you to the ten corresponding sources of academic innovations resembled in Figure 1.4.

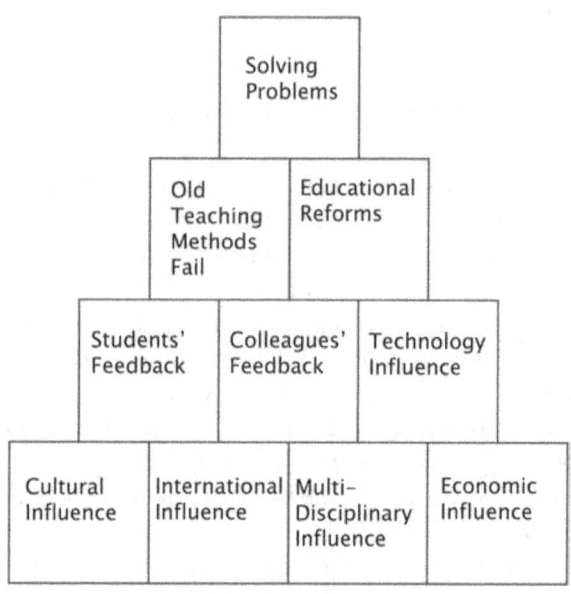

Figure 1.4:   Sources of academic innovations as a pyramid-shaped diagram.

1. **Solving problems** is a primary motivation of, and reason for design of new innovations. Problems often emerge in every course, in every classroom and in every educational system as there is no ideal educational system. The students' learning styles and their value orientations change from generation to generation. Students' preparation levels always vary from semester to semester, from year to year, from generation to generation and from culture to culture.

   In American universities, an example of such a problem is with basic arithmetic in many freshman level mathematics courses. To solve this problem, I decided include all the necessary transient algebra steps and provide students guided repetitive-type of examples where various algebra tricks emerge in different contents. Such problems with basic arithmetic can often prevent students from completing certain problems and lead them to a dead end.

2. **Old teaching methods** fail as each ideology has its' existing time limit. One particular example is the students' learning preferences seems to have shifted to a more applied basis instead of a traditional theoretical style of learning. "Real World" problems and examples are more readily understood and appreciated. In addition, during the last 20 years more students are using computers, cellular phones, and digital tablets in the classroom to take notes instead of writing on paper. Especially, easy access to instant information on the internet by using Google and Wikipedia and accepting what is presented as accurate has become a serious problem analogous to how calculators refrained students from determining answers on their own. Recently, more students miss classes to participate in conferences, competitions and prefer to take courses online remotely. This phenomena has frequently occurred in several educational systems.

    To keep with these changes, I decided to provide students course notes as pdf files and post them on MyCourses platform. This offers students opportunities to download the notes on their computers and follow them during the lectures instead of copying notes off the board. In addition, students will then have advance access to notes prior to the lecture and have access to the notes if they miss class for any reason.

3. **Educational reforms** occur quite frequently within universities and within educational systems. On one hand, educational reforms create inconveniences and challenges that require new courses and new teaching strategies. On the other hand, educational reforms lead to a strong motivation for innovation-oriented pedagogical activities in order to stay abreast of cultural changes and students' value orientations.

    Experiential learning is one of most recent academic reforms that occurred at RIT and other American universities during the last 20 years and offers students practical experiences such as undergraduate research opportunities and internships. I offered students open-ended questions to ponder about while teaching my undergraduate difference equations course at RIT and at the Aegean University in Greece. This exposed students to asking the right questions that guide them to new research discoveries.

4. **Students' feedback** is one of the most beneficial sources of academic innovations. Students often suggest new teaching strategies in their written evaluations such as using a digital tablet to teach an online course, providing more guided examples with more detailed explanations, posting notes on platforms prior to class, provide written comments on graded homework assignments and tests, and other analogous ideas. It is vital to be flexible to students' ideas and comments and understand why students suggest them.

   Providing a problem check list on tests was the very first suggestion that students recommended in my freshman Calculus courses. This serves as a navigation tool for students to keep track of what questions are solved and not to miss any questions on the test.

5. **Colleagues' feedback** is another essential source of academic innovations. Colleagues often see details that you do not necessarily see when they observe your class. It is also pertinent to listen to feedback after your presentation at a conference or during a casual pedagogical discussion. Their feedback and suggestions can guide you to recommend new courses, new seminars, new teaching strategies and to expand your teaching styles in new directions.

   My colleague from Riga Technical University department of engineering economics and management recommended me to teach a "Risk Management Seminar" for their students during our first meeting at a business conference. In addition, she encouraged me to conduct it as a multidisciplinary seminar and invite the Riga Fire Department to participate. The Fire Department shared about their practical experiences with taking preventive measures to reduce the risk of fire and enforcing fire safety laws. They also asked many questions about the American fire departments to gain cross-cultural comparisons between the American and the Latvian fire departments. This was a new frontier for me in teaching such a hands-on seminar. The professional/volunteer fire department's participation welcomed a new perspective to the seminar and a new interpretation to "Risk Management" which is often thought of in terms of finance instead of personal danger.

6. **Technology influence** also ignites new academic innovations as technology develops at a quite rapid paste. During the last 20 years, more students use computer equipment and various softwares as part of their learning process in comparison to the traditional learning style with paper and pencil. Students use technology to increase the speed of accessibility and exchange of information. Therefore it is vital to adjust the teaching styles together with technological enhances to accommodate the students' learning styles. This is especially pertinent in the online teaching and learning environment.

   Digitizing the practice work-sheets was one of the first beneficial technological feedback that students suggested in my SAT preparatory course at RIT. Students could practice solving the problems directly on their laptops and iPads and focus on solving practice problems instead of spending time copying problems from the board.

   In my online course that I recently taught at RIT, several students suggested to post the course notes on MyCourses platform in advance. This offers students opportunities to study the notes in advance and also follow the notes while I am teaching the material synchronously via Zoom.

7. **Cultural influence** entices new teaching innovations as well. Students in American universities nowadays are very active outside of class in various university clubs, societies, and other activities. Several university students participate in engineering competitions, undergraduate research, travel to conferences and other engaging and competitive events. It is therefore vital for faculty members to design a more flexible teaching style that will aid students with their activities as part of the university academic and cultural learning experiences.

   Several RIT students participate in undergraduate research conferences and in national engineering competitions. These students miss classes from time to time and will ask for an extension on homework assignments and for make up tests. These activities are an essential part of their practical and experiential learning and it is vital to support these students and be flexible with them by allowing them to hand in assignments late and take tests on different days and times.

Note that **Cultural influence** also involves collaboration, competition, hands-on projects, interaction with other students and learning past boundaries.

8. **International influence** certainly welcomes new academic innovations. Foreign students from different countries and cultures are often within any given American classroom and bring different learning styles and preparation levels that can be appreciated. This is a terrific opportunity for collaboration and cross-pollination through students working together and learning from one another. It can therefore be quite a challenge to adjust to multiple learning styles as students will focus on different details and ask different questions in comparison to American students. Being flexible with students and understanding why they ask specific questions is essential.

    In my freshman Calculus II online class, several foreign students ask more detailed questions on derivations of formulas in comparison to American students. In fact, they will pinpoint specific transient steps and ask for additional details beyond what I provide in the notes. American students will ask more detailed algebra questions when transient algebra steps are missing in the notes. Foreign students often detect more conceptual mistakes while the American students generally detect mistakes much faster than the foreign students.

9. **Multidisciplinary influence** is also a source of new academic innovations. For instance, students from numerous disciplines take freshman level courses such as Calculus and Discrete Mathematics. In these courses students have different learning goals, focus on different details and therefore ask different questions. Some of the students will focus on derivations and proofs and others will only focus on knowing how to apply the proved techniques. Furthermore, students from non-STEM disciplines also take some of these freshman level courses. This can certainly be quite challenging as the students' expectations vary.

    To balance out these contrasting differences, I design homework assignments with variations of difficulty levels in all my courses. I provide repetitive-type practice problems starting with the fundamental problems and then gradually transition to more challenging problems. Students with different backgrounds and preparation levels get a fair chance to grasp the concepts while working on each homework assignment.

10. **Economic Influence** has been a vital root of academic innovations as more students are working while taking courses. During the last 20 years more students take the advantage of co-ops, internships and fellow ships as part of their bachelor's program requirements. Some universities such as Drexel University and RIT require co-ops in some of their programs. This trend leads to designing a hand-on teaching and learning atmosphere and to offering more online courses for the students.

Starting with my freshman Calculus courses, to teach all my courses as more applied and hands-on, I redesigned my course notes by asking the right questions that stimulate new methods of solving problem and lead to new principles and applications. In my Discrete Mathematics course, I introduce Cartesian Product of sets and prime factorization that guide students to the basic principles of graph theory such as vertices, edges and the degrees of vertices. I also discuss applications in efficient computations and computer coding that helps students connect different concepts together and expand the range of applications.

The primary aim of new teaching innovations is to provide students a positive teaching and learning atmosphere inside and outside the classroom, make mathematics and international and multidisciplinary education accessible to everyone and to inspire students to learn. These fundamentals lead you to the upcoming section.

1.2 Positive Learning Atmosphere

A **positive learning atmosphere** for students is defined as a comfortable and flexible teaching and learning environment that leads to positive learning experiences and outcomes. The primary goal for each faculty member is to achieve the expected learning outcome while retaining a trustful and healthy relation with his/her students. This then directs you to the consequent three questions.

What does it take to achieve the expected learning outcome while providing a comfortable teaching and learning environment for the students? How do you navigate your students smoothly throughout the learning process and inspire students to learn? How do you make your course accessible for your students? Figure 1.5 addresses these three vital questions and presents the three essential modules that welcome the positive learning atmosphere and guides your students to positive learning outcomes.

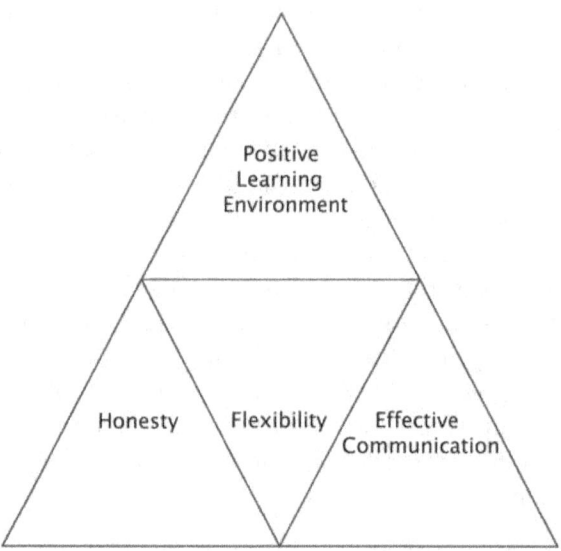

Figure 1.5: Positive learning environment as triangular-shaped structure.

1. **Honesty** is one of the first crucial modules in welcoming a positive learning atmosphere. First, if you are honest with students then students will be honest with you and trust you. Earning students' trust is vital for preserving the positive teaching and learning environment. This certainly includes fair grading and being honest about making mistakes. Honesty with students also minimizes the risk of plagiarism and cheating. Honesty with students leads to trust and to an amiable working environment.

   Providing written comments on each graded homework assignment and test demonstrates honesty to students as each student has a right to know what mistakes he or she made. Not only is it vital to be honest with students when you make a mistake in the notes, but to emphasize it and correct it. Recently I started giving each student five extra bonus points on a test for each mistake he/she detects. This certainly increased the trust level between me and my students.

2. **Flexibility** is another essential module in providing a positive learning atmosphere. Flexibility can be implemented with extensions of deadlines on assignments, re-submission of assignments, exchange of ideas and flexibility to students' feedback and suggestions. Students often think of alternative solutions, analyze problems from a different angle and see details that you may not see. In addition, students can recommend the use of specific technology and software for certain applications.

   Offering students flexibility on extensions on homework assignments alleviates students from extra stress and gives students additional time to absorb the concepts. This practice not only reduces the number of incomplete and blank assignments but increases the number of questions students started asking on homework assignments. Re-submission of homework assignments also increases the overall grade on homework assignments and the course performance.

3. **Effective communication** with students is also a pertinent factor that welcomes a positive and trustful learning atmosphere. For instance, immediate graded feedback serves as vital navigation tools for students that indicate where their mistakes are, what the mistakes are and how to correct their mistakes while the students' minds are fresh on the related content. Effective detailed answers to questions during class time help students to connect the concepts together and to see the sources of their mistakes and missing gaps. Prompt answers to questions by e-mail outside the classroom also contribute to the effective learning process.

   Students have perpetually commented that prompt and crisp answers to questions during class and by e-mail helped them clear up their ambiguities and grasp the concepts much faster and more effectively. Emphasizing the students' frequent mistakes also helps students detect the sources of their mistakes and how to correct them.

Supplemental attributes of these virtues will be discussed and how they direct to the development of new teaching techniques and development of new courses and seminars in latter chapters of the book. Positive teaching and learning environment then guides you to achieving the expected learning outcomes as well as exceeding the expected learning outcomes. Next, let's focus on multidisciplinary education.

1.3 Multidisciplinary Education

Multidisciplinary education studies, compares and coalesces two or more disciplines. In multidisciplinary education, two or more disciplines examine a specific topic from various unique perspectives and often with different utilizing techniques. In addition, multidisciplinary education compares similarities and differences in a specific theme and cross-cultural comparisons as well.

For instance, civil engineers and economists implement risk management with different applications; civil engineers apply risk management in studying mechanical failures while economists apply risk management in studying recessions and financial loses. Mathematicians and mechanical engineers write computer codes for numerical computations with different aims; mathematicians may write a code for numerical analysis while mechanical engineers many write a code for fracture analysis. Historians and political scientists analyze historical events with various outlooks; political scientists study more detailed events that occur in a shorter time frame in comparison to the historians who study a lengthier time period.

Multidisciplinary education can be a beneficial navigation tool to international education and collaborations as it explores a specific theme from various perspectives and examines cross-cultural comparisons. Figure 1.6 consists of two rows and presents five essential ingredients that animate and enhance Multidisciplinary education.

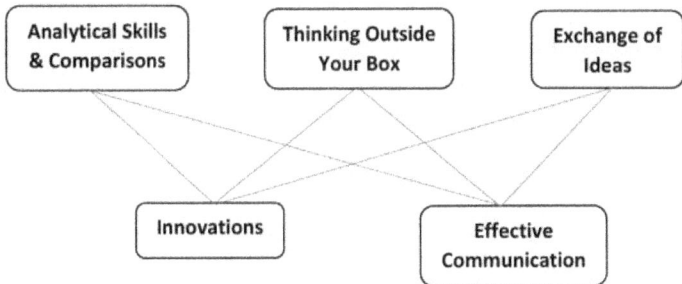

Figure 1.6: Bi-partite scheme of multidisciplinary education.

First we will focus on the concrete attributes of the three primary categories depicted in the first row in Figure 1.6.

1. Multidisciplinary Education develops and enhances **analytical skills and comparisons**. While studying two or more disciplines at the same time, it is vital to compare similarities and differences between disciplines. What are the similarities and difference between physics and civil engineering? What are the similarities and differences between history and political science? What are the similarities and differences between computer science and software engineering?

    I emphasize the importance of analytical skills and comparisons in my hands-on seminar on "Developing International and Interdisciplinary Research Coalitions" that I annually conduct at Riga Technical University Doctoral School and that I recently conducted in EKA University of Applied Sciences in Riga, Latvia. These serve as vital tools to developing new partnerships and innovations.

    In my Discrete Mathematics course, I expose my students to similarities and differences between the binary and the octal expansions, between the linear and geometric sequences, between permutations and combinations and between regular and semi-regular graphs.

2. Multidisciplinary Education leads to **thinking outside your box** or thinking outside and beyond your comfort zone. You encounter unfamiliar concepts and principles for the first time

that challenge your developed intuitions while studying additional disciplines which then direct you to new frontiers and to non-standard thinking and solutions to new encountered problems. Non-standard thinking then guides you to focus on concrete traits, to asking different questions and to asking the right questions.

In my seminar on "Developing International and Interdisciplinary Research Coalitions" and in my course on "Introduction to Business Start-Ups", I indicate that thinking outside your comfort zone and non-standard thinking is the first fundamental key factor to solving challenging problems that are beyond your experiences and intuitions and leads to new innovations. I also emphasize that we all encounter situations where thinking outside your comfort zone is not an option when you are assigned certain tasks and when solving specific problems.

3. Multidisciplinary education leads to **exchange of ideas** as people in different disciplines ask different questions, study different problems and have different experiences and intuitions. This guides you to the **holistic approach** that integrates various fragments from each discipline to formulate new questions and new ideas. For instance, mathematicians and anthropologists develop an extinction model, mathematicians and electrical engineers develop a neural networking model.

   I encourage my students to exchange ideas with me and with each other while solving multitasking problems. In my Discrete Mathematics course, students often recommend different approaches when determining cycles of graphs and chromatic number of graphs. In my Multi-variable Calculus course and Vector Calculus course, students exchange different ideas on how to determine partial derivatives and write double and triple integrals. In my seminar on "Developing International and Interdisciplinary Research Coalitions", I always encourage the participants to exchange ideas as I would like to learn from them as much as they would like to learn from me as they will have their own experiences to share.

Next, let's focus on the secondary categories in the second row of Figure 1.6.

4. Combination of items 1 and 2, 1 and 3, and 2 and 3 direct you to **effective communication**. Effective communication is essential in order to exchange ideas clearly while formulating new questions and attempting to solve new problems. In addition, effective communication is pertinent while analyzing and comparing contrasting views on a specific theme or problem. This is a pertinent skill as it prepares students for communication and collaboration with people with diverse backgrounds and prepares them to function in the professional world on the international and multidisciplinary level.

   Effective communication with students is not only essential while providing students graded feedback on homework assignments and tests, but it is just as essential while answering their questions. From my experience, it is vital to include as many details as possible and to provide similarities and differences with analogous concepts while answering students' questions.

5. Coalescing items 1 and 2, 1 and 3, and 2 and 3 also steer you to **Innovations**. Innovations often naturally emerge while exchanging ideas and analyzing similar and disparate concepts. Example of innovations are new seminars and courses within a specific discipline or multidisciplinary seminars and courses. It is not uncommon that a colleague from a different discipline will suggest a theme for a new seminar and course that may be beyond your experiences, intuitions and comfort zone.

   One of my colleagues asked me to conduct a "Risk Management Seminar" at Riga Technical University that I have never taught before. It turned out to be a very positive multidisciplinary learning experience as students from various disciplines and departments participate in this annual seminar. Furthermore, this seminar attracted participants from the Riga Fire Department.

   Even though I have never used a digital writing pad and pen before, one of my students asked me to start using a digital writing pad to answer questions more effectively in my online Calculus course instead of writing on paper and showing the solutions on paper through the camera. This increased the speed of communication with the students as students could ask more questions and could also save the files directly from the Zoom digital white board.

We will explore further features of these merits and how they can steer you to designing new international collaborations and innovations in latter chapters of the book. This then directs you to the expansion of international horizons.

1.4 Expansion of International Horizons

Expansion of international horizons often emanates naturally by colleagues' recommendations and suggestions. Also such opportunities can naturally arise after a specific international conference or an exchange program. At other times your curiosities, ambitions and adventurous traits can steer you to the expansion of new international horizons that offer new scopes and learning experiences.

Teaching abroad should be interpreted as a welcoming window and door of new opportunities to a new culture by comparing the similarities and differences between different educational systems, students' preparation levels, students' learning styles, and students' value orientations. Figure 1.7 traces six crucial integrants that welcome you to the discovery journey to expansion of international education.

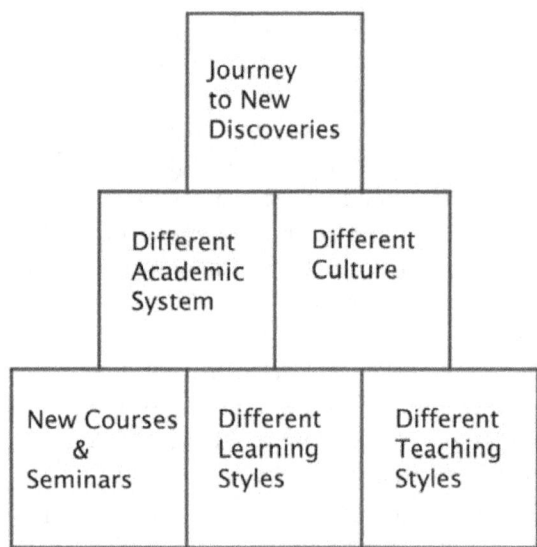

Figure 1.7: International pedagogy principles as a pyramid-shaped scheme.

1. International pedagogy can be interpreted as a **journey to new discoveries** as it guides you to new learning experiences in comparing similarities and differences in educational systems, cultures, students' preparation levels, students' learning styles, students' value orientations and making international education accessible to everyone. These traits often become natural sources to new academic innovations that can steer you to the design of modified courses and seminars and new courses and seminars.

    While spending time and teaching overseas during the last 12 years, my new colleagues at international and multidisciplinary conferences invited me to be one of the plenary speakers and suggested me to develop courses and seminars for their business programs. This was certainly a journey to new discoveries for me as I was only used to giving presentations related to mathematics and teaching math related courses.

2. International pedagogy welcomes you to a **different educational system** and directs you to the corresponding questions. What characteristics two academic systems share in common and what contrasting differences emerge? What teaching techniques work in both systems? What teaching techniques need adjustments that are geared to accommodate the essence of the new academic system? What new teaching innovations are needed to reach the expected learning outcome?

    While teaching my course on "Introduction to Recognition and Deciphering of Patterns" course for the high school students at Rezekne Technical Academy High School and while conducting Math Olympics in American Style for the high school students, I discovered that Latvian students were able to solve the same problems better and faster in comparison to the American students. This is due to students' preparation levels in the Latvian K-12 system that encourages students to compete and excel in mathematics and in STEM disciplines. The Latvian system also offers math summer camps for high school students.

3. International pedagogy also steers you be a part of a **different culture**, which then steers you to unique parental styles and students' value orientations, often quite different from your own. Traditional cultural values include family, friends, childhood, religion and commitment in achieving results (Platanova & Semyonov,

2018). Studies have illustrated that the students' value orientations vary and depend on the educational level, social status, regional factors, and membership in a national-ethnic group and religion (Kezina & Kondakov, 2015; Sukhina, 2015). Technology and globalization often affect the local culture and the students' value orientations.

One of the striking cultural differences that I discovered between the Latvian and the American educational systems is that more students in the American system ask questions in comparison to the Latvian system. In addition, students in the Latvian system were not as eager to answer questions in comparison to students in the American system.

4. Being a part of a different academic system and culture prompts you to design **new courses and seminars** that aid the students' preparation levels and yet challenges their intuitions and learning styles. Design of new courses and seminars helps you blend the two educational systems and cultures together and create a positive teaching and learning atmosphere and make international education accessible.

   Designing and teaching hands-on courses and seminars such as "Risk Management Seminar", "Developing International and Interdisciplinary Research Coalitions" and "Introduction to Business Start-Ups" opened new windows and doors of discoveries with cross-cultural comparisons between the Latvian, Ukrainian, Russian and Polish educational systems. In these courses and seminars, my students and I discuss the same questions with different experiences and approaches as the American and European economic and educational systems vary quite substantially, have different resources and have different financial infrastructures. The participants in these courses and seminars frequently ask me questions about the American economic and educational systems and the available resources.

5. Being acquainted with the students' **learning styles** is crucial while designing new courses and seminars. Understanding the students' learning styles steers you to the students' intuition, background and preparation levels. These are vital sources to focus on when teaching specific themes and how much details to include.

Students' learning styles can arise as a cultural phenomena or as an individual phenomena (Jerkins, 1991).

While teaching my courses and seminars in Latvia and Ukraine I discovered that students ask specific questions based on their learning styles and based on their value orientations and hence focus on specific details. These questions are related to available resources and financial models and constraints. High school students gravitate to asking questions related to proof techniques.

6. The new or adjusted **teaching style** for each designed course and seminar will vary depending on the students' preparation levels and their learning styles. In some instances it is enough to modify a specific teaching strategy and in other instances a new teaching style will be necessary in order to achieve a certain learning outcome. While attempting to match new teaching style and learning style, it is essential to retain the cultural balance and preserve certain traits of your teaching style. Matching teaching and learning styles? This question was studied by Gayle V. Davidson (Davidson, 1990).

As I was teaching my Introduction to Discrete Mathematics course at the Transportation and Sakaru Institute in Riga, Latvia, I did make several adjustments such as offering students consultation hours on weekends, by Skype and cellular phone. However, I did retain my American teaching characteristics by asking students questions, providing students hands-on practice problems during class time, assigning weekly homework assignments and giving tests every 3–4 weeks.

Rebekah Glebe encourages international pedagogy as it is a journey to new discoveries of new multidisciplinary collaborations and innovations (Glebe, 2020). On one hand, challenges will emerge at times past your experiences and comfort zones. Such challenges can be cultural differences, cultural barriers, misunderstandings, rejected innovations, unsuccessful implementations of innovations, etc. On the other hand, such challenges should be interpreted as positive learning experiences that welcome non-standard approaches to solving new unfamiliar problems and are a welcoming window and door of new opportunities and innovations to promote international and multidisciplinary education and practices.

Prior to designing new mathematics and multidisciplinary courses and seminars, it is crucial to establish a base of successful teaching strategies for various courses.

1.5 Summary

Discovering new international frontiers will present you rewards and challenges. International frontiers will widen your horizons and comfort zones and welcome you to new innovations and communication skills and problem solving techniques. Breaking cultural barriers will be one of the challenges that will require you to think outside your comfort zone, experiences and intuitions. Figure 1.8 evokes strong currents and waves in the mighty Atlantic Ocean in Cape Hatteras, North Carolina.

Figure 1.8: The mighty Atlantic Ocean in Cape Hatteras, North Carolina.

What essential experiences and techniques do you need to apply to break through the waves and sail across the mighty Atlantic Ocean?

1.6 Further Thoughts

1. I successfully taught the Graduate Record Examination (GRE) preparatory course at RIT for 12 years. Several students from Latvia come to the U.S. for graduate studies and must take the GRE. Why I could not convince the administration to offer the GRE preparatory course for students in Latvia?

2. I successfully taught the "Introduction to Recognition and Deciphering of Patterns" course for high school students at the Rezekne Technical Academy High School in Latvia. How do I market and expand this course in other high schools in Latvia and in other countries?

3. I developed the course on "Introduction to Business Start-Ups". Why none of the universities in Latvia were interested in it but it sold successfully in some of the universities in Ukraine, Poland and Russia?

4. After conducting "Math Olympics in American Style" event at the University of Latvia in Riga, Latvia, one participating student came up to me asked me of I could teach a course for high school students in her high school. I contacted the school principle and the potential idea vanished without a trace? Why did this happen?

Chapter 2

Mathematics Teaching Strategies

This chapter's goals are to conceive a foundation of successful mathematics teaching tactics that are often initiated by new academic reforms, cultural changes, technological advances and international influences. New teaching tactics are devised to solve problems that frequently occur in courses that you teach and to enhance the students' performance. Andreas J. Stylianides and Gabriel J. Stylianides recommend classroom intervention as a teaching tactic in mathematics education (Stylianides & Stylianides, 2013). New pedagogical innovations often emerge naturally by recycling previous ideas and asking the related questions resembled in Figure 2.1.

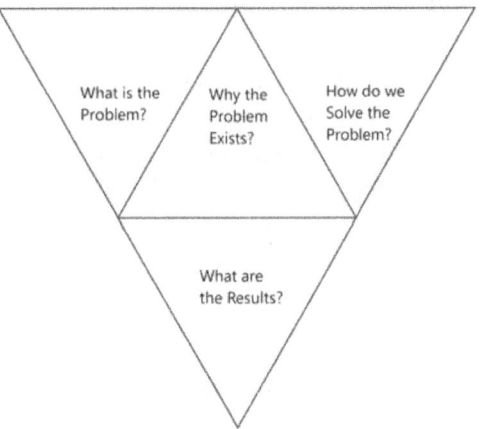

Figure 2.1: Foundation of tactics in triangular-shaped form.

Figure 2.1 presents the characteristics of the four key questions that guide you to new teaching tactics and innovations.

1. **What is the problem** is the first vital question to address when you design new teaching tactics. Asking this question becomes the first source to developing a new pedagogical innovation to address a specific problem. For instance, problems with recursive sequences and with proof by induction in Discrete Mathematics.

2. **Why the problem exists** is the next crucial question to ask. Determining the root(s) of the problem is inevitable in order to commence with new ideas. The problem with recursive sequences in Discrete Mathematics exists as students do not have enough exposure and experiences with formulating various sequences analytically such as linear, quadratic, geometric and recursive sequences.

3. **How do we solve the problem** is the third vital question to direct. To solve the problem with recursive sequences in Discrete Mathematics, the introduction to patterns and additional practice problems was vital. This was not a part of the course curriculum but aided as a transient tool to enhance the students' intuitions.

4. **What are the results** is the final question to convey. Did the students get a better grasp on recursive sequences? Do they see more details than before? Do they see the transition from one term to the next?

Mark Keane advocates the use of analogs as a potential strategy to solve a problem (Keane, 1987). This section's aims are to examine seven new developed teaching tactics: Hands-on teaching and learning, repetitive-style problems, use of multiple colors (four color technique), posting notes and videos on platforms, multiple re-submissions of homework assignments, prompt feedback and flexibility to students' feedback. Section 2.1 will focus on hands-on teaching and learning.

2.1 Hands-on Teaching and Learning

One of the key factors of teaching innovations in the American educational system is to design a more hands-on teaching and learning atmosphere in and outside the classroom (Hake, 1998). The goals of the hands-on teaching tactic is to present abstract concepts as more concrete and to increase the students' academic performance. Therefore, the hands-on teaching and learning is an activity-oriented teaching style (Ekwueme *et al.*, 2015). The first vital question to address: How do you enact these new ideas and innovations (Shields, 2003)? Many American universities such as Drexel University and the Rochester Institute of Technology offer undergraduate engineering programs that require co-ops and internships by working in a company or for a government agency for at least one semester as part of the graduation requirements. Several business programs also started offering hands-on education with many hands-on analysis courses. How do you proceed with the hands-on education beyond the scopes of the engineering programs? Can you implement this strategy in mathematics and in other disciplines? The first row in Figure 2.2 describes the three primary traits of the hands-on teaching and learning.

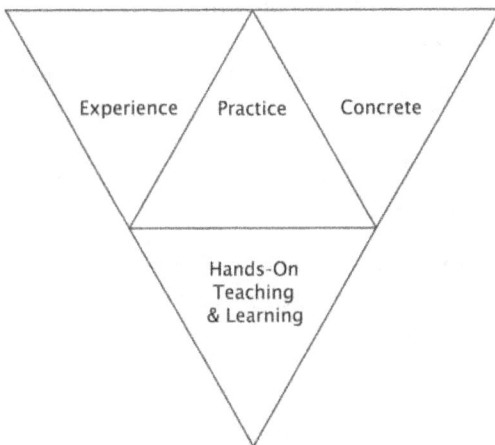

Figure 2.2: Hands-on teaching and learning in triangular-shaped guise.

As resembled in Figure 2.2, the hands-on teaching tactic leads to knowledge by experience and practice and offers concrete representations of concepts. Next, let's focus on the concrete features of the three primary categories resembled in the first row of Figure 2.2.

1. **Experience** is the first vital feature of the hands-on teaching and learning tactic. This learner-centered tactic allows the learner to see, touch and manipulate objects while learning. Many American

universities offer courses and programs with experiential learning that offer students practical experiences.

The College of Engineering at the Rochester Institute of Technology offers students practical learning experiences outside the classroom with co-ops and internships, participation in undergraduate research conferences and participation in engineering competitions by designing racing cars and boats. Business schools in several eastern European countries such as Poland, Czech Republic, Ukraine and Latvia offer practical working experience for students in local banks, hotels, restaurants, etc. Students gain practical learning experience in parallel to the principles they learn in their courses.

2. **Practice** is the next essential feature of the hands-on teaching and learning tactic. This learner-centered tactic provides students opportunities to practice solving problems in the classroom.

   Students in all my math courses that I teach at RIT and in Latvia gain practical experiences in solving math problems during class time. In fact, my students receive immediate feedback on their progress and get additional chances to detect and correct their mistakes. Students in my "Risk Management Seminar" that I conduct annually at Riga Technical University gain practical experience in constructing the risk matrices that estimate the risk and active participation in discussions.

3. **Concrete representation** of the content is also a pertinent feature of the hands-on teaching and learning tactic. It communicates the principles more effectively in comparison to theoretical representation of the content.

   High school students in my "Introduction to Recognition & Deciphering of Patterns" course experience analyzing and formulating different patterns that emerge from various geometrical configurations such as system of pyramid-shaped squares at the same scale, system of diminishing squares, system of 45−45−90 triangles at the same scale, piece-wise functions, etc. Students also experience formulating theorems and proving them by induction.

Sections 2.1.1–2.1.3 will examine specific categories of hands-on teaching and learning practices such as repetitive-style problems, extensions and multiple re-submissions of homework assignments, and posting notes and videos on platforms. Section 2.1.1 will focus on **repetitive-style practice problems**.

2.1.1 Repetitive-Style Practice Problems

Repetitive-style practice problems is the first example of a hands-on teaching tactic. Repetitive-style practice problems involve repetitions of identical or similar contents. These may include repetitions of sentences in a foreign language, repetition of a musical cadence and repetition of solving linear equations in algebra. This re-emphasizes the principle "Practice Makes Perfect".

Repetitions can serve as a very vital tool in implementing successful teaching and learning styles. In fact, repetitions perform as a very crucial fragment during the learning process when studying music and learning to play a musical instrument, when studying a foreign language, and during sports practices (Murgulis, 2012; Yakovlev & Yakovleva, 2014). In addition, psychologists sometimes analyze thousands of repetitions in particular behavior(s) before coming to any conclusions. Furthermore, the department of transportation analyzes repetitions of traffic patterns numerous times before any decisions are made to do any construction projects.

Repetition is also an essential resource in teaching and learning as students start to detect their mistakes after solving several repetitive types of problems. Furthermore, teachers start to detect students' frequent mistakes after solving several repetitive-type problems, can emphasize the common mistakes to their students and recognize the differences in the students' varying learning styles (Grasha & Yangarber-Hicks, 2000; Iyer et al., 2001).

Now, let's transition to sharing about successful practices in implementing the repetitive-style practice problems in Calculus, SAT preparatory course, and in Discrete Mathematics. My first encounter with this practice commenced during my first semester at RIT while teaching freshman Calculus. In fact, this practice was part of the **workshop-based Calculus** with bi-weekly workshops that provided students repetitive-style practice problems. For instance, the **Quotient Rule** is used to determine each derivative as the expressions emerge in the quotient form.

1. $\frac{d}{dx}\left[\frac{x^2}{x-1}\right]$,
2. $\frac{d}{dx}\left[\frac{x}{x^2+1}\right]$,

3. $\frac{d}{dx}\left[\frac{\sin(2x)}{1+\cos(2x)}\right]$,

4. $\frac{d}{dx}\left[\frac{e^{-x}}{1-e^{-x}}\right]$.

Implementing this tactic helped me detect students' frequent mistakes during class and workshops and on their homework assignments. After implementing this tactic, students started asking more questions and provided positive and supportive evaluations as it helped improve their overall course performance. After implementing this technique in my freshman Calculus courses, I then decided to implement this tactic in my SAT preparatory course. This led me to design work-sheets with repetitive-type problems for the SAT preparatory course similar to the ones in Project-Based Calculus courses. The four repetitive-type problems below focus on factoring or expanding **quadratic equations**.

1. What is the value of k if $(t-12)$ is a factor of $t^2 - kt - 48$?
2. What is the value of $x^2 y - xy^2$ if $xy = 8$ and $x - y = 10$?
3. What is the value of $(x+y)^4$ if $x^2 + 2xy + y^2 = 4$?
4. What is the value of xy if $(x+y)^2 = 64$ and $(x-y)^2 = 36$?

This tactic also helped me monitor students' frequent mistakes and gave me chances to provide students more accurate and precise feedback after the students solved each problem. On the contrary, this helped students stay focused on the material in a very intense two and a half hour class (Orlova & Radin, 2018). Recently I had the opportunity to implement this strategy in my Discrete Mathematics course. The four repetitive-type problems below focus on **formulating summations in the sigma notations**.

1. $4 + 8 + 12 + 16 + \cdots + 240$,
2. $1 + 3 + 5 + 7 + \cdots + 45$,
3. $4 + 16 + 36 + 64 + \cdots + 900$,
4. $1 + 2 + 4 + 8 + \cdots + 1{,}024$.

Section 2.1.2 will focus on extensions and multiple re-submissions of homework assignments.

2.1.2 Extensions and Multiple Re-Submissions

Extensions on homework assignments and multiple re-submissions of homework assignments are additional examples of successful hands-on teaching tactics. First, these tactics reduced the students' stress level and offered students opportunities to grasp the material and concepts at their own pace (Radin & Shlat, 2021). Second of all, this reinforces the repetitive-style teaching and learning practice outside the classroom (Orlova & Radin, 2018). Based on the students' repeated comments in their evaluations, extensions on homework assignments and multiple re-submissions of homework assignments present the following advantages and positive characteristics:

1. Offers students flexibility to grasp the concepts at their own pace.
2. Encourages students to ask questions as they are attempting to understand the sources of their mistakes.
3. Students start to see the sources of their mistakes and gaps that occur during the learning process.
4. Offers students opportunities to catch up if they are falling behind with keeping up with the assigned course pace.
5. Making the course accessible to many students and offers a more amiable teaching and learning atmosphere.

Furthermore, after implementing these pedagogical tactics, students' performance increased by 20% and more students wrote positive and supportive comments in their teaching evaluations (Orlova & Radin, 2019; Radin & Shlat, 2020). We will address how these tactics are implemented in the online teaching and learning atmosphere in Chapter 8. Section 2.1.3 will focus on posting notes and videos on platforms.

2.1.3 Posting Notes and Videos

Posting notes and videos on various platforms such as MyCourses, Google Drive, Microsoft Cloud, etc. is another example of a successful hands-on teaching tactic. Analogous to Section 2.1.2, this strategy also offers students opportunities to grasp the material and concepts at their own pace and reinforces the repetitive-style teaching and learning practice outside the classroom (Radin & Shlat, 2020). Posting notes and videos present the following advantages and positive features:

1. Offers students opportunities to stay abreast if they miss class.
2. Look at the material as many times as necessary to grasp the concepts and see the connections between the concepts.
3. Students can learn the material on their own prior to the lectures and ask more detailed questions during lectures.
4. Offers a more amiable teaching and learning atmosphere for foreign students and students with disabilities as they have the flexibility to have unlimited access to notes and videos outside of class.

After posting notes and videos, the students' performance increased by 20% and more students wrote positive and supportive comments in their teaching evaluations (Orlova & Radin, 2019; Radin & Shlat, 2020, 2021). In Chapter 8, our aims are to address how these tactics are implemented in the online teaching and learning atmosphere. Section 2.2 will examine the **use of multiple colors** technique.

2.2 Use of Multiple Colors

Colors are a vital part of the learning environment and process as colors have a subterranean consequence on how people feel both psychologically and physically as colors represent different moods. Color is one of the effective factors in a space which influences the way individuals express their emotions (Kingsley, Osueke & Kurt, 2014). Certain colors are more commonly associated with a given concept (Beck, 1960). This section will focus on using colors to distinguish different patterns, different regrouping of terms and decomposition of fragments.

I perpetually used different colors in all my courses that I have taught over the last twenty years and students frequently called it **the four-color technique** in their evaluations. This technique worked successfully for the first time when teaching the product rule, quotient rule and chain rule of differentiation in freshman Calculus course. This technique also worked effectively when adding and multiplying unlike patterns while solving recursive sequences. This technique was especially essential while teaching graph theory by indicating different degrees of vertices of graphs, determining the chromatic number of graphs, decomposing outer edges and inner edges of graphs, and presenting different cycles of graphs.

Now I would like to take the opportunity to share about this technique that I recently implemented in Introduction to Recognition and Deciphering of Patterns course that I taught for the high school students at the Rezekne Technical Academy. The first example describes a piecewise sequence decomposed into a blue even-indexed sequence and a green odd-indexed sequence:

$$2,\ 4,\ 6,\ -8,\ 10,\ 12,\ 14,\ -16, \ldots$$

$$\{x_n\}_{n=0}^{\infty} = \begin{cases} 2(n+1) & \text{if } n = 0, 2, 4, 6, \ldots, \\ (-1)^{\frac{n-1}{2}}[2(n+1)] & \text{if } n = 1, 3, 5, 7, \ldots. \end{cases}$$

The upcoming sketch decomposes a piecewise function into a system of blue diagonal lines with a positive slope and a system of green diagonal lines with a negative slope:

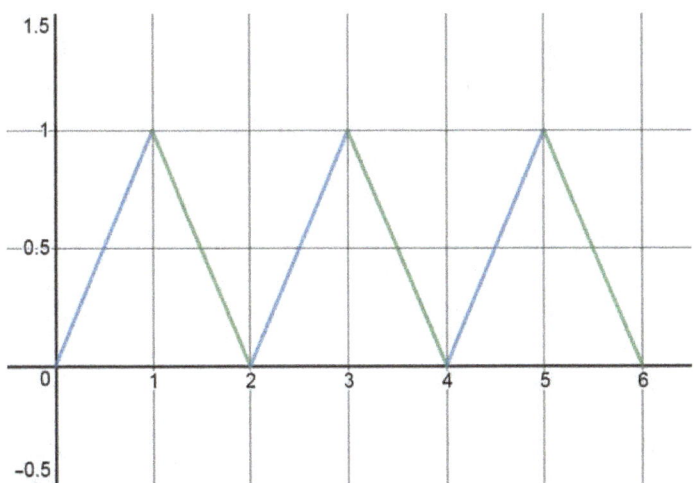

The succeeding picture resembles a system of shrinking squares and circles; blue diminishing squares and green diminishing circles:

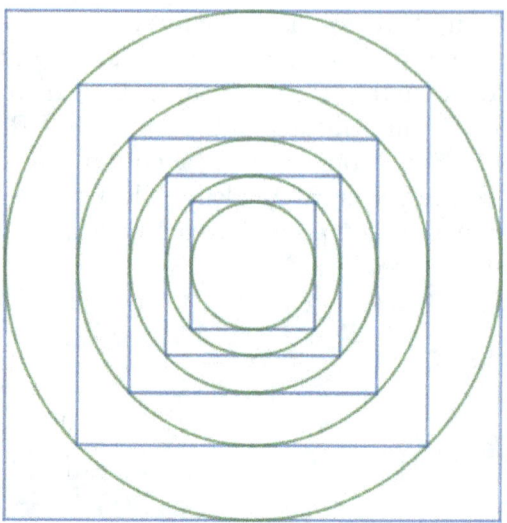

The next diagram renders the use of the lower-triangular method of grouping the entire sum into three different summations and three corresponding colors to prove a specific characteristic of the Pascal's triangle:

$$\binom{4}{0}$$

$$\binom{4}{1} + \binom{4}{1}$$

$$\binom{4}{2} + \binom{4}{2} + \binom{4}{2}$$

$$\binom{4}{3} + \binom{4}{3} + \binom{4}{3} + \binom{4}{3}$$

$$\binom{4}{4} + \binom{4}{4} + \binom{4}{4} + \binom{4}{4} + \binom{4}{4}$$

The upcoming sketch presents the shades of blue to emphasize the system of shrinking sub-triangles inside the primary triangle, where the larger size triangles emerge in lighter shades of blue and the smaller size triangles emerge in darker shades of blue:

Section 2.3 will focus on **Prompt Feedback**.

2.3 Prompt Feedback

Feedback is an essential part of the learning process in any context. **Formative feedback** is a constructive feedback and is used to improve teaching and learning. **Summative feedback** is the final judgment of the student's achievement (Asmar *et al.*, 2014). Feedback should serve as a positive navigation guide instead of a negative and punitive method. Feedback should indicate where exactly the mistake occurs and why the mistake occurs. Providing prompt and detailed feedback is an essential part of the learning process with the corresponding advantages and positive attributes:

1. The students' minds are still fresh on the current material and it is easier for the students to understand and correct their mistakes.

2. Provides students enough time to understand and correct their mistakes before an exam.

3. Steers students in the right direction and prevents students from making similar mistakes in different contents. Prevents the domino effect of mistakes.

4. Provides swift and efficient communication between students and the professor.

5. Provides a positive and trustworthy teaching and learning atmosphere.

After implementing prompt feedback, the students' performance increased by 20% and more students wrote positive and supportive comments in their teaching evaluations (Orlova & Radin, 2019; Radin & Shlat, 2020, 2021). We will address how these tactics are implemented in the online teaching and learning atmosphere in Chapter 8. Section 2.4 will guide you to examine how **flexibility to students' feedback** welcomes new improvements and new innovations.

2.4 Flexibility to Students' Feedback

Not only feedback is an essential part of learning for the students, but it is just as essential for the faculty members too. The first step in becoming a innovator is to carefully analyze the students' feedback from the course evaluations (Herman, 2011). In fact, if several students write the same comment or similar comments, do they have good intentions to suggest future improvements in the course and in other courses (Smallbone & Quinton, 2010)? Are there good reasons, especially if the same comment or similar comments appear on the evaluations during different semesters or during consecutive semesters (Hussain & Khan, 2016)? My students frequently mentioned the following suggestions on their teaching evaluations:

1. Digitizing the work-sheets in SAT preparatory course presented students the advantage to concentrate on practicing problems instead of spending time copying the problems from the board. The students found the class to be more effective and productive.

2. Providing hands-on practice problems during class time in upper level courses.

3. Posting pdf files and the corresponding video files in online courses helped students follow the videos easier while looking at both files at the same time.

4. Using the digital writing tablet and the Zoom white board in online courses was an effective communication tool during office hours to work out and emphasize all the vital details.

5. Posting homework assignment deadlines, test dates, and homework assignments using the MyCourses platform instead of sending numerous e-mails to students.

6. Providing prompt feedback and prompt answers to e-mails helps students to grasp the concepts.

2.5 Summary

Developing new teaching strategies is vital to solve certain problems, to make the course more accessible, to create a welcoming and amiable teaching and learning atmosphere and to achieve the expected learning outcomes. Figure 2.3 paints the mountainous landscape with multiple crests in the Colorado Rockies in Rocky Mountain National Park.

Figure 2.3: The mighty mountainous crests in Rocky Mountain National Park.

Figure 2.3 also invites you to discover new alpine destinations with their unique rocky miens and characteristics.

2.6 Further Thoughts

1. In Section 2.1.2, we discussed about extensions on homework assignments and multiple re-submissions of homework assignments. This strategy worked successfully in my mathematics courses. Can this strategy be applied successfully in business courses and humanities courses? What possible problems and challenges can arise and how to handle them?

2. In Section 2.2, we discussed about the use of multiple colors together with decomposition into different groups. What is the recommended number of groups and colors that is comprehendible to students? Should you use different colors or various shades of a specific color?

3. In Section 2.4, we discussed the importance of flexibility to students' feedback. From time to time, students ask me to post solutions on all the homework assignments and tests. Is this a good idea? What are the advantages and disadvantages of this?

4. In Section 2.1.1, we discussed how effectively the repetitive-style practice problems can work. How do we balance the difficulty level of problems while implementing this technique?

Chapter 3

Expansion of International Horizons

Why expand your international horizons? This chapter's aims are to present motivations and inspirations to teach abroad which then pilot you to the expansion of international horizons. It is an exciting and yet a challenging discovery journey that welcomes you to new cultures from which you develop new experiences based on the established experiences and intuitions and often forces you to think outside your comfort zone. Extended international travels broaden your global perspectives and help you stay abreast of various changes such as educational reforms and changes in students' learning styles. Thus, it is vital to adjust to these changes and provide students with contemporary information literacy, pedagogical literacy, organizational literacy and temporal literacy (Briere et al., 2012). Extended international travels broaden your global perspectives and can promote new collaborations and hence influence new teaching styles and innovations (Radin & Riashschenko, 2017). For instance, after his lengthy travels in China, Marco Polo introduced gun powder and pasta to Europe that instantly ignited many technological and culinary innovations and changes throughout Europe.

This chapter will focus on comparing various educational systems, building international relations, promoting new courses and seminars, making international education accessible and utilizing resources. The upcoming section will examine similarities and differences between educational systems.

3.1 Comparing Educational Systems

You can discover numerous similarities and differences while observing and photographing marine sunsets in different seas and oceans. The first photograph captures the Baltic golden sunset in Liepaja, Latvia.

Figure 3.1: Baltic Golden Sunset.

The second photograph renders the Aegean golden sunset in Santorini, Greece.

Figure 3.2: Aegean Golden Sunset.

Figures 3.1 and 3.2 both capture the sunset's golden phase. The Aegean gold in Figure 3.2 traces a brighter shade of gold in comparison to the Baltic gold in Figure 3.1 as the Aegean Sea is much saltier than the Baltic Sea. Second of all, Figure 3.2 has no cloud cover and was taken at a higher altitude above sea level, where Figure 3.1 has significant cloud cover and was taken at sea level. Also observe that Figure 3.1 has much bigger waves in comparison to Figure 3.2 and therefore paints a darker tone of gold.

The upcoming sequence of photographs will compare marine landscapes along the mystic Baltic Sea in Liepaja, Latvia and along the mighty Atlantic Ocean in Cape Hatteras, North Carolina. The first photograph paints the clouds, the golden sand and the turbulent Baltic theme along the shores of Liepaja, Latvia.

Figure 3.3: Waves along the Baltic shores of Liepaja.

The second photograph resembles the clouds, the golden sand and the turbulent Atlantic theme along the shores of Cape Hatteras, North Carolina.

Figure 3.4: Waves along the Atlantic shores of Cape Hatteras.

Figures 3.3 and 3.4 both capture the white clouds, golden sand, shades of green and blue water and the white turbulent waves. In Figure 3.3, the clouds reflect brighter shade of white and the sand depicts a more dazzling scope of gold in contrast to Figure 3.4. On the other hand, Figure 3.4 renders a brighter and more aggressive tone of white of the Atlantic waves and the green and blue Atlantic waters in contrast to Figure 3.3. This occurs due to the higher concentration of salt along the Atlantic shores in Cape Hatteras in comparison to the Baltic shores in Liepaja and due to deeper water along the Atlantic shores.

Akin to distinguishing the similarities and disparities of golden sunsets in Figures 3.1 and 3.2 and marine landscapes in Figures 3.3, 3.4, 1.1 and 1.2, we can detect parallel contrasts between two academic systems. Analogous to Figure 1.3, Figure 3.5 models what similar traits two academic systems share in common and what distinct features each academic system offers.

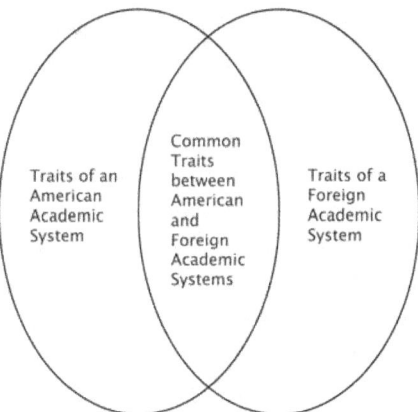

Figure 3.5: Academic systems' features as a venn diagram.

Comparing similarities and differences between academic systems enhances your analytical skills and critical thinking skills. Second of all, this is also essential for future improvements and innovations in your courses and seminars that you regularly teach as it opens new windows and doors of perspectives by introducing new ideas and practices from one system to another. Here are several examples of such exchanges between the American, Greek, Latvian and Ukrainian academic systems:

1. I taught an analogous course on "Introduction to Research in Difference Equations" at the Aegean University in Samos, Greece during my spring 2009 sabbatical after teaching "Introduction to Difference Equations" at Rochester Institute of Technology.

2. After teaching "Introduction to Discrete Mathematics" at Rochester Institute of Technology, I taught an analogous course on "Discrete Mathematics for Electronics Engineering" at the Transportation and Sakaru Institute in Riga, Latvia during my spring 2016 sabbatical.

3. I developed and taught a new course on "Introduction to Recognition & Deciphering of Patterns" for high school students at the Rezekne Technical Academy High School in Rezekne, Latvia after teaching "Introduction to Discrete Mathematics" at the Rochester Institute of Technology (RIT). I also wrote a textbook on this topic.

4. After conducting the "MATHBOWL" olympics event hosted by the RIT K-12 office for high school students, I designed and conducted an analogous event "Math Olympics in American Style" event for high school students in Latvia hosted by the University of Latvia Department of Mathematics.

5. I developed a new course on "Introduction to Business Start-Ups" that I taught at the Academician Yuriy Bugay International & Scientific Technical University in Kiev, Ukraine after conducting the seminar on "Developing International & Interdisciplinary Research Coalitions" at Riga Technical University and at EKA University of Applied Sciences in Riga, Latvia.

6. After teaching the "SAT Preparatory Course" at RIT and after conducting "Math Olympics in American Style" event for high school students in Latvia, I developed a new course on "Introduction to Math Olympiad" and wrote a textbook on this topic.

Next, we will decipher similarities and contrasts between the American, Latvian, Polish, Ukrainian, and Hungarian academic systems. What do the American and Polish K-12 academic systems have common and what disparities exist between the two systems? The American and the Polish K-12 systems both teach foreign languages. However, the Polish system has special language schools where students start to learn English, German or French in second grade, where American students start to learn a foreign language in seventh grade at the earliest.

Another striking difference between the American and the Polish systems is that Polish high schools offer students a choice between a general lyceum, a vocational education and a technical secondary school. This will depend on the results of the compulsory exam that must be taken at the end of a year where Polish students could qualify and continue their high school education and study 3–4 years in high school. From vocational studies alone, Polish students could already earn what is called a vocational diploma and start to work.

What do the American and Ukrainian academic systems have in common and what discrepancies arise between them? To answer this question, let's focus on the university undergraduate admissions systems. Both systems require students to take the university admission exams and examine the students' high school grades.

In the Ukrainian system, students can choose specific state universities depending on the results of their admission test. In addition, the results of the admission test is a determining factor if a student will be awarded free education or "budget place" or will have to pay for the education. There are several private universities in Ukraine that offer equivalent education but not free of charge in comparison to the state universities.

In the American education system, the SAT scores is also an essential determining factor whether a student will get accepted to a specific university. However, once a student is accepted to a state or private university, he or she will have to pay the university tuition unless a scholarship or financial aid is awarded. Akin to the Ukrainian undergraduate admission system, the doctoral programs in American universities also offer students teaching and research assistantships and free tuition depending on their GRE scores and their grade point average.

What do the American and Hungarian academic systems have in common and what deviations emerge between the two systems? First, let's focus on the K-12 systems. Both systems offer 8 years of primary school plus 4 years of high school till age 18. However, the Hungarian system offers three main types of high schools. The "gymnasium" which primarily prepares students for university level education and two types of vocational/technical schools which prepares student for different types of jobs (similar to the vocational diploma in the Polish system). Teachers pushing students into the direction where their talents lie describes the traits of the Hungarian system.

Next, let's examine the American and Hungarian university systems. Both systems offer bachelor's, master's and doctoral programs. Medical school, law school, and teacher training are the exceptions. The current Hungarian university system is organized by the "Bologna System" with 3 years for a bachelor's, additional 2 years for a master's, and 4–5 more years for a doctorate. In Hungarian universities, students are either subsidized by the state or they pay; this depends on the students' preparation level and on their entrance exam result.

What do the American and Latvian academic systems have in common and what differences occur between them? Both K-12 systems offer 12 years of education and both systems teach mathematics, foreign languages and science. However, the Latvian K-12 system covers the material at a greater depth and prepares students for national and international competitions, which is part of the Latvian culture. This is also due to fact that the American K-12 system over-focuses on getting students to do well on the standardized exams. I personally experienced witnessing these results after conducting the "MATHBOWL" event hosted at RIT and the "Math Olympics in American Style" hosted by the University of Latvia department of mathematics.

Parallel to the Hungarian and Ukrainian universities, students in Latvian system are either subsidized by the state or they pay, which also depends on the students' preparation level and on their entrance exam result.

Detecting these similarities and contrasts between the American and foreign educational systems is a crucial navigation tool that will accurately guide you to new international collaborations and to the development of revised and new seminars and courses. Figure 3.6 portrays the percentage of acceptance rates to universities in various countries.

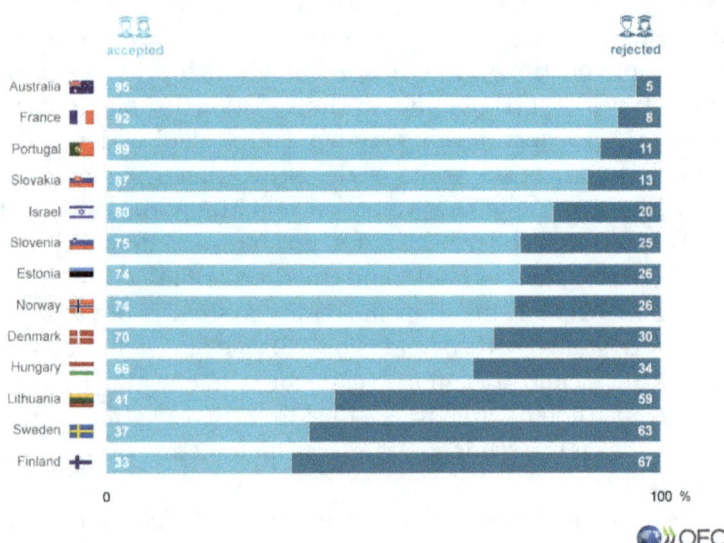

Figure 3.6: Percentage of acceptance rates.
Source: Education indicators in focus N°63.

3.2 Building International Collaborations

International collaborations often naturally arise while expanding international horizons and while comparing educational systems. Expansions of international horizons and comparison of educational systems are an invitational journey to new discoveries, experiences and ventures. For instance, while I spent my first sabbatical at the Aegean University in Greece, the Island of Samos revealed its' unique Aegean-marine landscape presented in the corresponding two photographs in Figures 3.7 and 3.8.

Figure 3.7:   Alpine Landscape on the Island of Samos in Greece.

Figure 3.8: The Aegean green shores on the Island of Samos in Greece.

Even though I have seen numerous marine landscapes along the Atlantic Ocean, the Pacific Ocean, the Baltic Sea, the Black Sea, the Caribbean Sea, and the Adriatic Sea, the Island of Samos attracts its' unique Aegean-marine landscape with special scopes of green, blue and white and its' unique island alpine landscape as you can see in Figures 3.7 and 3.8. In order to appreciate such pearls, it is vital to be vigilant in the new environment and be flexible to new discoveries. Moreover, it is essential to compare the similarities and differences relative to your current knowledge, experiences and intuitions.

While traveling, participating in international conferences, exchange programs and in international sabbaticals you can encounter numerous new academic and professional opportunities. Analogous to discovering Aegean-marine landscape in Figures 3.7 and 3.8, you can discover new research directions, new seminars and courses to teach which lead you to new innovations and publications. This is summarized by the cognate rhombus diagram in Figure 3.9.

Figure 3.9: Academic and professional opportunities rhombus model.

1. Active participation by asking the right questions during international conferences, sabbaticals and exchange programs can lead you to new research directions, new seminars and courses to design and teach.

   During the International Scientific Symposium "Economics, Business & Finance", in Jurmala, Latvia a colleague invited me to design and conduct a "Risk Management Seminar" at Riga Technical University department of Engineering Economics and Management. During the Society, Integration, Education International Scientific Conference in Rezekne, Latvia a colleague invited me to design and teach a course on "Introduction to Recognition and Deciphering of Patterns" for high school students at the Rezekne Technical Academy High School.

2. New research directions often result in new publications and in new innovations.

   My colleague and I from University of Latvia published several manuscripts on periodic character on piecewise difference equations after she invited me to do research in this new direction; this guided me to write a new textbook on "Periodic & Eventually Periodic Solutions of Max-Type and

Piecewise Difference Equations". My colleagues and I from Yaroslavl State University published several manuscripts on economic cycles after they invited me to do research in this new direction. These new collaborations not only lead to new publications but also lead to new research questions and innovations. My colleague from RUDN University in Moscow, Russia invited me to do research on financial forecasting.

3. Conducting new seminars often guides you to new publications and to new innovations.

   After conducting my "Risk Management Seminar" at Riga Technical University I was invited to do research in Disaster Planning and Management. After conducting my seminar on "Developing International and Interdisciplinary Research Coalitions" at Riga Technical University I developed a new course on "Introduction to Business Start-Ups".

4. Designing and teaching new courses often guides you to new publications and to new innovations.

   After teaching my course "Introduction to Recognition and Deciphering of Patterns" at Rezekne Technical Academy High School, I wrote a textbook on this topic that I plan to use in future new developed courses. After teaching this course, I developed a new course on "Introduction to Math Olympiad" for high school students. Furthermore, after teaching my course on "Applications of Difference Equations in Robotics" at Riga Technical University during my spring 2016 sabbatical, a student invited me to conduct research in Modeling Human Emotions.

3.3 Promoting New Seminars and Courses

Design and promotion of new seminars and courses are often naturally born as international collaborations develop. Developing and promoting new seminars and courses can be a new and challenging learning expedition. As an experienced hiker, I explored the beautiful and yet challenging alpine landscape of the Canadian Rockies and the Colorado Rockies described in Figures 3.10 and 3.11.

Figure 3.10: Alpine landscape in Banff National Park.

Figure 3.11: Alpine landscape in Rocky Mountain National Park.

In Figure 3.10 the Canadian Rockies in Banff National Park reveal an alpine landscape with numerous shades of green. On the other hand, in Figure 3.11 the Colorado Rockies in Rocky Mountain National Park resemble a more course alpine landscape with higher altitudes and various tones of white. As an experienced hiker and mountaineer, what inspires you to discover new alpine terrain? How do you plan these new expeditions? What new outcomes do you plan to achieve?

Analogous to planning alpine expeditions to explore new mountainous frontiers, Figure 3.12 reveals the related vital questions you must ask while you are developing and promoting a new course or seminar in a different academic system.

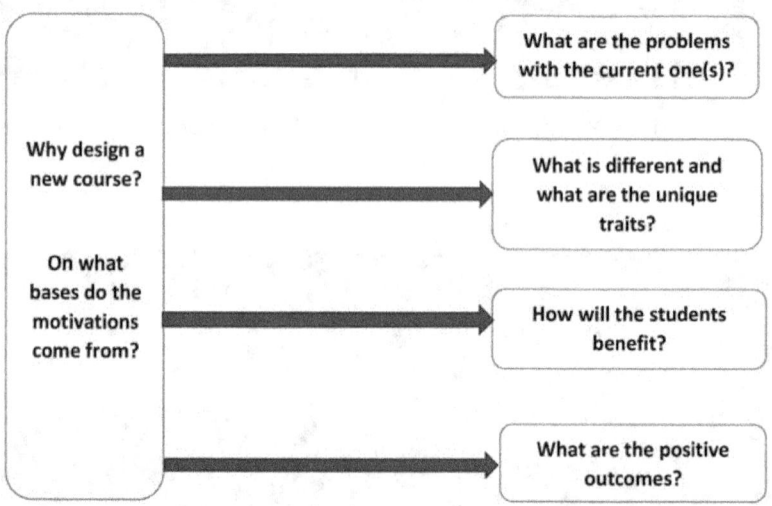

Figure 3.12: Essential questions for designing a new course or seminar.

1. The first vital question to ask: Why design a new course in a new academic system? There are many motivations that give such a push: New course based on previous course(s), recommendation from a colleague, recommendation from a student, exploring new frontiers in a new academic system, promoting your teaching principles in a new academic system, promoting your knowledge in a new academic system, etc.

    The second essential question to ask: What are the bases or origins of motivations? Most of the seminars and courses you design originate from previous seminars and courses that you have taught once upon a time or from a seminar or course that you participated in.

I designed my course on "Introduction to Math Olympiad" based on my SAT Preparatory course, on my Discrete Mathematics course and on my course on Introduction to Recognition and Deciphering of Patterns. I designed my course on "Introduction to Business Start-Ups" based on my seminar that I conducted on "Developing International and Interdisciplinary Research Coalitions" and based on my international collaborations that I successfully established.

2. These questions then guide you to the next vital question: What are the problems with the current one(s)? A specific course may be very successful and well liked by the students but it is never perfect. They maybe problems with some of the contents, some topics may not be covered in great depth and some pertinent topics may be missing that could be of paramount importance and interest.

In my Discrete Mathematics course, there is not enough time to delve into depth of fundamentals of sequences, summations and properties of the Pascal's triangle due to the problem with quite many topics and not enough time. In addition, the course does not cover topics such as piecewise sequences and piecewise functions. This was my primary motivation to design a course on "Introduction to Recognition and Deciphering of Patterns" that I taught for the first time for the high school students at the Rezekne Technical Academy High School in Rezekne, Latvia.

3. This then leads you to the next essential question: What is different and what are the unique traits? This is especially important when you are writing a proposal for such a course and seminar. These questions are very important to address in order to prevent any serious overlaps and conflicts of interest with existing courses and seminars.

The questions about the difference with similar courses and the unique traits emerged while I was designing my course on "Introduction to Business Start-Ups" before it was approved by my colleagues at the Academician Yuriy Bugay International & Scientific Technical University in Kiev, Ukraine.

4. Next, let's address the corresponding questions. How will the students benefit from the course or seminar? What new perspectives, outlooks and skills will the students gain?

While I taught my course on "Introduction to Recognition & Deciphering of Patterns" for high school students at the Rezekne Technical Academy High School, students have been exposed to a large percentage of the material. However, my course welcomed them to much bigger depth of the concepts that they have not yet experienced. In fact, the students encountered new techniques to solve specific problems.

5. What are the positive outcomes?

In my seminar on "Developing International & Interdisciplinary Research Coalitions", students gained new outlooks and perspectives on how to effectively communicate and build new partnerships. Furthermore, students gained new outlooks on how to efficiently use available and limited resources.

3.4 Available Resources

Available resources are a vital factor in the successful development and implementation of new courses and seminars. The cognate cyclical diagram in Figure 3.13 presents frequent resources that you will encounter while designing a new course and seminar.

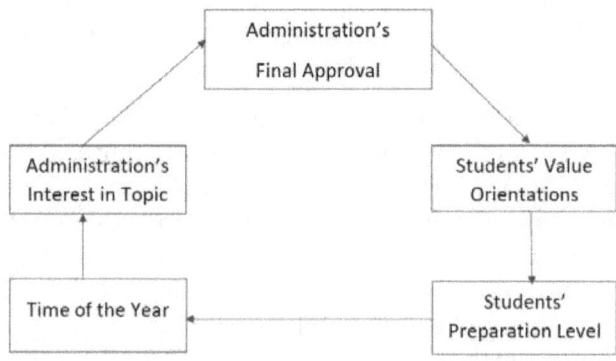

Figure 3.13: Cyclical diagram of resources.

Therefore, before and while designing a specific course or seminar it is essential to keep these factors in mind.

1. The first vital resource to contemplate is the **students' value orientations**. This specific resource gives clues to what contents that you design in a course and seminar.

    I implemented the students' business orientations in starting their own business while I devised my online university level course on "Introduction to Business Start-Ups" at the Academician Yuriy Bugay International & Scientific Technical University in Kiev, Ukraine. In fact, I designed it as an applied hands-on course that steers the students to problem solving, non-standard thinking and to asking the right questions.

2. The next essential resource to consider is the **students' preparation level**. This concrete resource gives clues to what level of difficulty of the contents that you can design in a course and seminar.

    I designed my high school level course on "Introduction to Recognition & Deciphering of Patterns", with no pre-requisites that welcomed students to analyzing patterns, formulating patterns and proofs. The course started off on the elementary level and the difficulty level gradually progressed.

3. **Time of the year** is also another pertinent resource for you to think about when developing a new course and seminar. Fall, spring or early summer. This is when the students' schedules could be the most accommodating.

    I drafted my university level seminar on "Developing International & Interdisciplinary Research Coalitions" at Riga Technical University. As a 2-day seminar, the supervisor and I decided that the best time to conduct it was during the break between the end of the spring semester and the final exams. This is a break for the students that accommodated their schedules.

4. **Administration's interest in the topic** or **convincing the administration** that the course or seminar will benefit the students and them is certainly an important factor for you to keep in mind while developing a new course and seminar.

    While drafting my university level seminar on "Developing International & Interdisciplinary Research Coalitions", I successfully convinced my supervisor that this will be beneficial to the students. Students often meet foreign colleagues at conferences and while traveling and this is a good way to start potential collaborations.

5. **Administration's final approval** is the most vital resource. This may require several revisions before the final approval is granted after convincing the administration that the course or seminar will benefit them and the students.

While devising my university level "Risk Management" seminar at Riga Technical University, my supervisor recommended me to make several revisions such as risk of fires prior to conducting the seminar for the first time.

More details on resources such as limited resources and maximizing success within limited resources will be discussed in Chapter 6.

3.5 Summary

Expansion of international horizons enhances your multi-cultural, multidisciplinary comparison and communication skills. It also welcomes you to new educational systems and heightens your analytical skills. Figure 3.14 greets the volcanic formations and the shades of green and blue of Lago de Fuego on the Island of Sau Miguel, Portugal.

Figure 3.14: Lago de Fuego on the Island of Sao Miguel, Portugal.

Sau Miguel is the largest island among the Azores Islands. Figure 3.14 paints the alpine landscape with special shades of Azorian green and blue.

3.6 Further Thoughts

1. According to Figure 3.12, one would like to design a new course on International Pedagogy. What questions will this course address?

2. According to Figure 3.13, the students were interested in a new course and asked a faculty member to teach it. For what reasons did the administration was not interested in the theme?

3. According to Figure 3.13, the administration was interested in the topic for a new course. For what reasons did the administration did not give final approval for the course?

Chapter 4

New Mathematical Horizons

This chapter will focus on expanding your mathematical horizons by asking the corresponding questions: Why expand your mathematical horizons? Why design your new math courses and seminars in different academic systems? Why design your new math courses and seminars in different academic systems in an online environment? Why explore your new destinations beyond the horizon?

Figure 4.1: Marine Horizons in the Baltic Sea.

It is natural human curiosity to discover new destinations. Discovery of new destinations is a learning process as you gain new perspectives while traveling and comparing similarities and differences. You will also expand your bases of knowledge and intuitions. For instance, after his long international travels, President Theodore Roosevelt established the system of national parks in the U.S. which is appreciated nationally and internationally to this day.

Figure 4.2 resembles the rudiments of mathematics horizons.

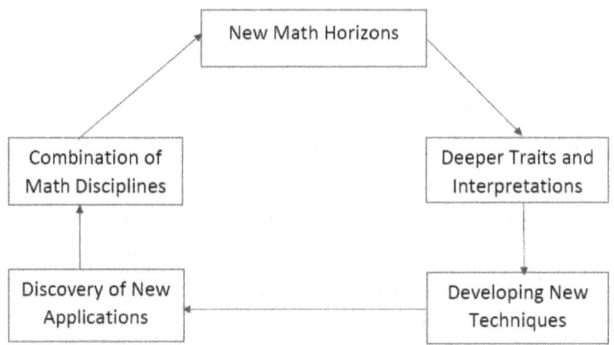

Figure 4.2: Rudiments of mathematical horizons.

1. New mathematical horizons will guide you to **deeper interpretations** of well studied concepts that you have been exposed to numerous times.

   Getting acquainted with deeper details of solving linear and nonlinear difference equations led me to design a new course on Difference Equations and also to write several textbooks related to difference equations.

2. **Deeper interpretations** will then lead you to the **development of new techniques** of formulations and proofs.

   I developed new techniques in formulating sequences, summations and for algebraic proofs and for proof by induction while preparing lessons for Discrete Mathematics course.

3. **The development of new techniques** will often direct you to create **new applications** of well studied concepts.

   While designing my course on "Introduction to Recognition & Deciphering of Patterns" I discovered applications of sequences and summations in various geometrical configurations. Figure 4.3 traces a system of shrinking squares.

Figure 4.3: System of shrinking squares.

The dimensions of the squares in Figure 4.3 is described by a geometric sequence.

4. Discoveries of new applications then navigates you to **combinations of math disciplines**.

    While constructing my digital work-sheets for my SAT Preparatory Course, I applied combinations of several math disciplines to effectively solve multi-step and multi-tasking problems such as: Solving exponential equations, angular geometry, geometry and percents, word problems with decomposition, word problems with rates, properties of integers, etc.

You gain new perspectives while you are developing new courses. The upcoming Sections 4.1–4.6 will share about the discoveries of mathematical horizons.

4.1 Workshop-Based Calculus at RIT

Teaching **Workshop-Based Calculus** as a new faculty member at RIT was one of my first mathematical innovation discovery journeys. The course was designed with weekly workshops that provided students hands-on practice problems. The primary objective of this pilot course was to improve students' performance, to improve the students' retention rate and lower the students' failure rate at RIT. Contriving the workshops was an innovative challenge for me as I was new to this pilot teaching practice.

To meet the pilot's objectives, I decided to include repetitive-type practice problems with varying levels of difficulty. In addition, I included a diversity of different topics on each worksheet. I included a few questions on topics that have not yet been taught yet. The corresponding list of repetitive-type practice problems provides students opportunities to gradually grasp **Integration By Parts**:

1. $\int xe^{2x}\ dx$,
2. $\int x^2 e^{-x}\ dx$,
3. $\int arctan(x)\ dx$,
4. $\int x^2 Ln(x+1)\ dx$,
5. $\int \frac{x^3}{(x^2+1)^3}\ dx$.

Figure 4.4 describes the advantages of the workshop-based Calculus pilot.

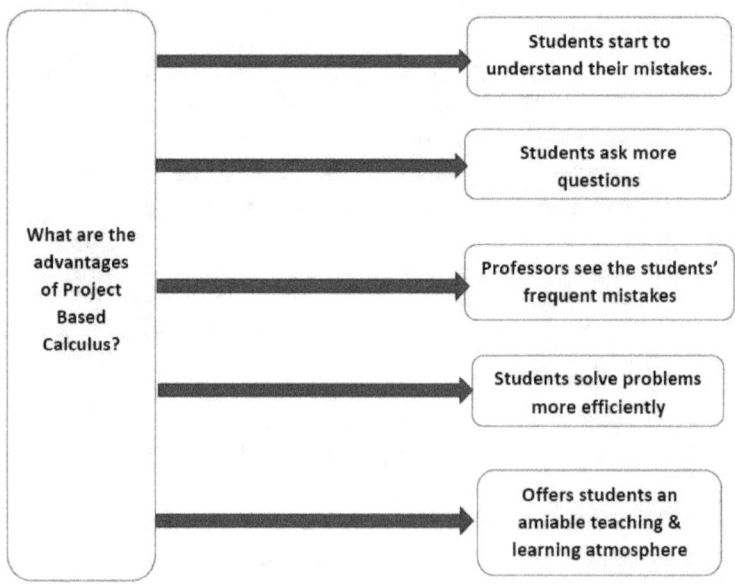

Figure 4.4: Advantages of workshop-based Calculus pilot.

I had the opportunity to teach workshop-based Calculus in an online environment and more details will be discussed in Chapter 8. The remaining sections will focus on using similar pilots to make mathematics accessible, offer students an amiable teaching and learning atmosphere and achieve and go beyond the learning outcomes.

4.2 SAT Preparatory Course

The aim of the 5-week **SAT preparatory course** that RIT offers is to train high school students to solve problems correctly and efficiently and to do well on the SAT exam. Analogous to workshop-based Calculus, I decided to design the course as a hands-on course by providing students workshops with practice problems. Akin to Figure 4.4, students gained practice in solving problems while I monitored their frequent mistakes.

The course's aims are to recognize various categories of topics and to recognize distinct patterns. This trick worked well to get students to solve problems correctly and efficiently within the limited time that they are given on the real SAT exam. The corresponding set of problems address **Geometry and Proportions**:

1. Suppose that 80% of the rectangular area is 120 square feet. Determine the area of the entire rectangle.

2. In a rectangle $\square ABCD$, point E is the midpoint of $\overline{BC}$. If the area of ABED is $\frac{2}{3}$, what is the area of rectangle $\square ABCD$.

3. Consider a rectangle that is 15 inches long and 10 inches wide. Suppose that rectangle is enlarged with a constant ration such that the width becomes 22 inches wide. Determine the new length of the enlarged rectangle.

4. Suppose that a farmer has two rectangular fields. The larger field has twice the length and four times the width. If the smaller field has area K, then the area of the larger field is much larger than the area of the smaller field.

These set of problems not only provide good practice for students but also offers me opportunities to monitor if students take much longer to solve a specific problem than the expected time. I can then detect specific reasons why these problems occur and navigate students in the right direction how to solve these problems more efficiently.

4.3 Discrete Mathematics

After teaching workshop-based Calculus and the SAT preparatory course at RIT with hands-on repetitive style, I decided pilot this practice while teaching Discrete Mathematics at RIT. The course's objectives are to recognize when and how specific patterns emerge. Similar to workshop-based Calculus, I designed the course with hands-on practice problems during class time. Analogous to Figure 4.4 students not only gained practice in solving problems while I monitored their frequent mistakes but also recommended alternative solutions to various problems. The associated set of problems address **Graph Theory** questions:

1. Determine how many edges must be removed in a simple k-regular graph with n vertices to produce a spanning tree.
2. Sketch $L_{4,6}$ and sketch a Hamiltonian cycle of $L_{4,6}$.
3. Determine for what value of n and m the bi-partite graph $K_{n,m}$ has an Eulerian cycle.
4. Determine the maximum number of edges of a regular graph **G** with 8 vertices where $\chi(G) = 2$.

I also had the opportunity to implement this pilot practice while teaching Introduction to Discrete Mathematics for Electronic Engineers at the Transportation & Sakaru Institute (TSI) in Riga, Latvia. The strategy worked really successfully. However, the primary difference is that the Latvian students worked in groups in comparison to American students working individually. Table 4.1 presents the students' evaluations from the spring 2016 Discrete Mathematics course taught at TSI.

Table 4.1: Spring 2016 semester students' evaluations at TSI.

Teacher/ Subject	Object Content acc. describing Objects	Course contents are not duplicates another item	Their subject matter the teacher explained clearly	Recommended reading materials are easily accessible and useful	Test work during the semester whether the subject development	The teacher was available on the consultation	I would love to listen to more of any course in this teacher	Teacher's explanations on the results of verification activities were sufficient
Michael Radin	4.91	4.91	5.00	4.55	4.91	4.80	4.91	4.82
Discrete Mathematics	4.91	4.91	5.00	4.55	4.91	4.80	4.91	4.82

Furthermore, I had the opportunity to teach Discrete Mathematics in an online environment and more details will be discussed in Chapter 8. This will then guide you to the remaining sections that will focus on international math horizons.

4.4 Introduction to Difference Equations

While teaching Complex Variables at RIT, several students asked me to teach a specialized course on Difference Equations. I then decided to develop undergraduate and graduate level courses on Difference Equations with hands-on teaching and learning style. Similar to workshop-based Calculus and Discrete Mathematics, the students had opportunities to solve problems during class time. The associated set of problems address **First Order Linear Difference Equations**:

1. Show that $x_n = \frac{8^{n-2}}{5^{n-1}}$ satisfies the given Δ.E.:
$$5x_{n+1} - 8x_n = 0.$$

2. Solve the given **initial value problem**:
$$\begin{cases} 3x_{n+1} + 5x_n = 0, & n = 0, 1, \ldots. \\ x_0 = -\frac{27}{5}. \end{cases}$$

3. Solve the given **initial value problem**:
$$\begin{cases} x_{n+1} = x_n + n^2, & n = 0, 1, \ldots. \\ x_0 = 0. \end{cases}$$

4. Determine the existence and pattern of periodic solutions of:

$$x_{n+1} = -a_n x_n + 1, \quad n = 0, 1, \ldots,$$

where $\{a_n\}_{n=0}^{\infty}$ is a period-2 sequence.

Students were required to do a research project in the graduate level course. The project required students to analyze long-term behavior of a specific difference equation by analyzing the boundedness character, periodic nature and convergence. I offered students opportunities to present the results of their research projects on a weekly basis during the last 4 weeks of the semester. Students not only presented their results by providing graphics but also asked each other questions and provided each other constructive criticism and feedback.

After teaching Difference Equations at RIT, I decided to teach an analogous graduate level course at the Aegean University in Greece during my spring 2009 sabbatical. This was also a hands-on and research oriented graduate level course. Students met with me one-on-one to discuss the progress on their project and presented their results in class as well.

In comparison to the American students, the Greek students were a bit more loathed to present their results in a group setting and preferred to present it individually in my office. In addition, the Greek students needed a little bit more guidance with their research projects in comparison to the American students.

4.5 Recognition and Deciphering of Patterns

Teaching Discrete Mathematics at RIT and at the Transportation & Sakaru Institute and teaching Difference Equations directed me to design and teach a new course on "Introduction to Recognition & Deciphering of Patterns" for Latvian high school students. I used Discrete Mathematics and the fundamentals of Difference Equations as a base and added more topics such as piecewise functions, summations and applications of sequences and summations in geometrical configurations. I chose this theme after the principle of Rezekne Technical Academy High School asked me to teach a math course for his high school students. The course has the following objectives for the students:

1. To make mathematics accessible to high school students.
2. To introduce university level mathematics to high school students.
3. To gain practice in recognizing and deciphering various patterns.
4. To strengthen experiences and intuitions in observing, recognizing and generalizing patterns.
5. To enhance students' proof by induction techniques.

Figure 4.5 traces an **ascending step-shaped period-4 cycle**.

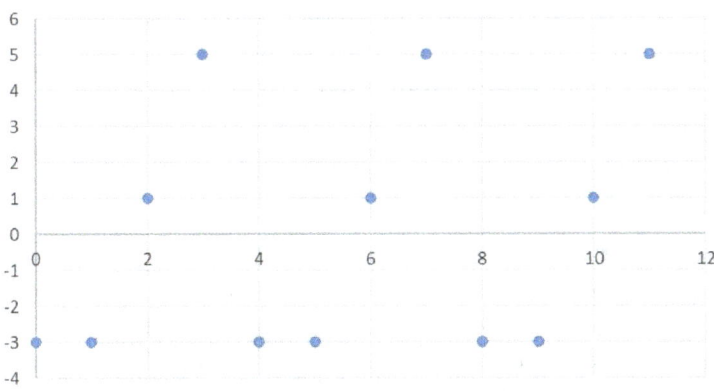

Figure 4.5: Ascending step-shaped period-4 cycle.

Note that the period-4 cycle in Figure 4.5 also emerges as a hockey stick. The corresponding set of problems lead to the proofs of **Pascal triangle's characteristics**:

1. For $k, n \in \mathbb{N}$, prove:
$$\binom{n}{k} + \binom{n}{k+1} = \binom{n+1}{k+1}.$$

2. For $n \geq 2$, prove:
$$\binom{n}{n-2} + \binom{n+1}{n-1} = n^2.$$

3. For $n \in \mathbb{N}$, prove:
$$\sum_{i=0}^{n} \binom{2n+1}{i} = 4^n.$$

4. For $n \geq 2$, prove:

$$\sum_{i=0}^{n-1} \binom{i+1}{i} = \binom{n+1}{n-1}.$$

4.6 International Math Olympiad

This section will describe various events related to math olympics. These will include sponsored math olympics events in the U.S. and in Latvia, a designed course in math olympics, textbook on math olympics and statistical charts from International Math Olympiad. Section 4.6.1 will focus on Math Olympics in American Style Event.

4.6.1 *Math Olympics in American Style*

My encounter and journey with Math Olympics commenced by conducting the MATHBOWL event hosted by the RIT K-12 program. I designed and conducted this event with five rounds, where each round has 12 multiple choice questions. Students from six different school districts participated in this annual event.

After conducting the MATHBOWL event at RIT, I suggested to my colleagues at the University of Latvia Department of Mathematics to host a similar event. I decided to name it "Math Olympics in American Style" as the event originated from the U.S. I then assembled this event with seven rounds. The first six rounds have 12 multiple choice questions. The last round has 12 open-ended questions. Close to 100 students participated in this annual event from 16 different school districts throughout Latvia.

For both events, I constructed questions from numerous topics such as factoring, percents, average value, geometry, word problems, properties of integers, fundamentals of numbers, sequences, etc. The following are sample questions from the events:

1. If $m > 0$ and x is $m\%$ of y. In terms of m, y is what percent of x?

2. Suppose that line ℓ passes through the origin and is $\perp$ to the line $4x+y=k$. If two lines intersect at the point $(t, t+1)$, then determine t.

3. Suppose that the average of the tests in the first class of k students is 70. Next, suppose that the average of the tests in the second

class of n students is 92. When the scores from both classes is combined the total average is 86. What is the value of $\frac{n}{p}$?

4. If x is equal to the sum of even integers between 10 and 60 inclusively, and y is the number of even integers between 10 and 60. What is the value of $x+y$?

The questions for both events were similar. However, quite many contrasting differences occurred between the two events:

1. The MATHBOWL event was conducted as an evening event in comparison to "Math Olympics in American Style" that was conducted as an all day event.

2. Latvian students generally answered questions much faster in comparison to the American students.

3. Latvian students generally lasted much longer by answering all the questions correctly in the first three rounds in comparison to the American students.

4. Latvian students generally had much stronger preparation in comparison to the American students.

4.6.2 *Introduction to Math Olympics*

Teaching my SAT preparatory course, conducting MATHBOWL and "Math Olympics in American Style", and preparing students to compete in Math Olympics, directed me to write a textbook on "Introduction to Olympiad Problems" and to design a course on "Introduction to Math Olympics".

The objectives of this course is to get students acquainted with the fundamentals of sequences, summations, geometry, number theory, set theory, graph theory, Pascal's triangle, proofs and proof by induction, etc. The knowledge of these fundamentals will also guide students to solving more challenging problems. The corresponding problems are sample questions:

1. Solve the following **initial value problem**:

$$\begin{cases} x_{n+1} = 2^{2n+1} x_n, \\ x_0 = 1. \end{cases}$$

2. For $n \geq 2$, **prove** that the sum of $2n+1$ consecutive integers is a multiple of $2n+1$.

3. Determine the ending digit of 72^{75}.

4. For $k \geq 1$, prove that $6^k - 1$ is divisible by 5.

5. Prove that $4^2 - 2^2, 10^2 - 8^2, 16^2 - 14^2, \ldots$ are divisible by 3.

4.6.3 Results of International Math Olympiad

The first international Math Olympiad was held in Romania in 1959. In the U.S., the first Math Olympiad events were hosted in 1977 by Dr. George Lenchner (an internationally known math educator). Currently, many regional, national and international Math Olympiad events are held annually worldwide. Figures 4.6 and 4.7 present the results of countries' performances from the international Math Olympiad events. Figure 4.6 presents the winner frequency of certain countries.

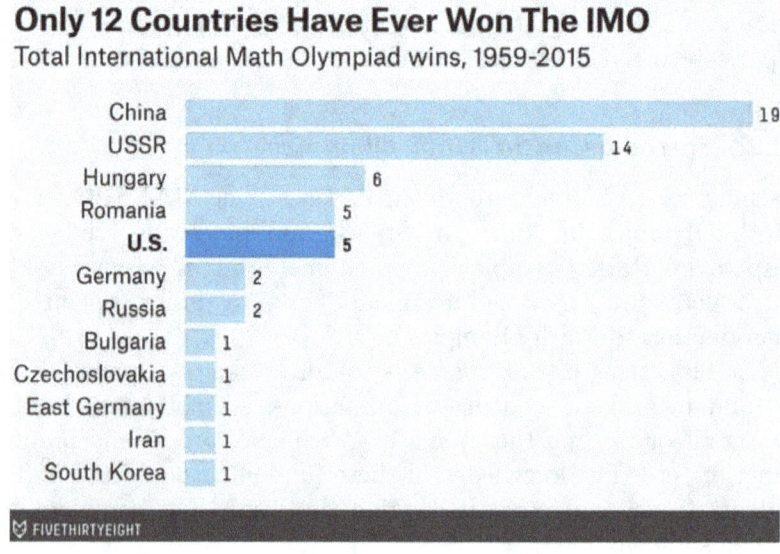

Figure 4.6: International Math Olympiad-winner frequency.
Source: International Math Olympiad.

Figure 4.7 portrays the performance of specific countries from 1990 to 2020.

Figure 4.7: International Math Olympiad-performance of countries.

4.7 Summary

New mathematical horizons present you new latitudes such as alternative thinking and creative methods to analyzing and solving problems. They also welcome you to new teaching practices and amiable teaching and learning environment. Figure 4.8 reveals a system of canyons at diminishing scales.

Figure 4.8: System of canyons at diminishing scales.

Figure 4.8 also traces a fractal-shaped structure of system of canyons.

4.8 Further Thoughts

1. In Section 4.1, we discussed the hands-on practice for students. Will this strategy work for all students? What are the disadvantages of this?

2. In Section 4.2, we discussed the digitizing of notes to refrain from copying notes off the board. What are the disadvantages of this?

3. In Section 4.6.1, we discussed the introduction of new style of conducting Math Olympics. What are the potential obstacles that you can encounter in other countries?

4. In Section 4.6.2, we discussed the introduction of teaching the fundamentals of math olympics. Will this strategy work for all the students and will this strategy work in all academic systems?

Chapter 5

New Multidisciplinary Horizons

This chapter will focus on developing and expanding your multidisciplinary horizons. Multidisciplinary horizons analyze two or more disciplines and address the following questions: Why multidisciplinary horizons emerge naturally? Why are multidisciplinary horizons important? Why develop your multidisciplinary horizons? Why expand your multidisciplinary horizons in an online environment? How multidisciplinary horizons guide you to further international collaborations? (see Figure 5.1).

Figure 5.1: Alpine Horizons in the Canadian Rockies.

Multidisciplinary collaborations widen your bases of knowledge, intuitions, horizons, enhance your problem solving techniques and welcome new international frontiers. Multidisciplinary collaborations and horizons also compare what two disciplines have in common and their contrasts. On one hand, the upcoming photograph depicts the hilly landscape of the Blue Ridge Mountains in Virginia (see Figure 5.2).

Figure 5.2: Blue Ridge Mountains' hilly landscape.

On the other hand, the succeeding photograph describes the dunes' hilly formations along the Baltic Sea in Latvia (see Figure 5.3).

Figure 5.3: The dunes' hilly landscape along the Baltic Sea.

Note that Figures 5.2 and 5.3 both describe the hilly miens formed by the winds. However, the alpine terrain in Figure 5.2 is composed of different material and is much bigger magnitude than the Baltic dunes in Figure 5.3. The succeeding diagram in Figure 5.4 resembles the fundamentals of multidisciplinary horizons.

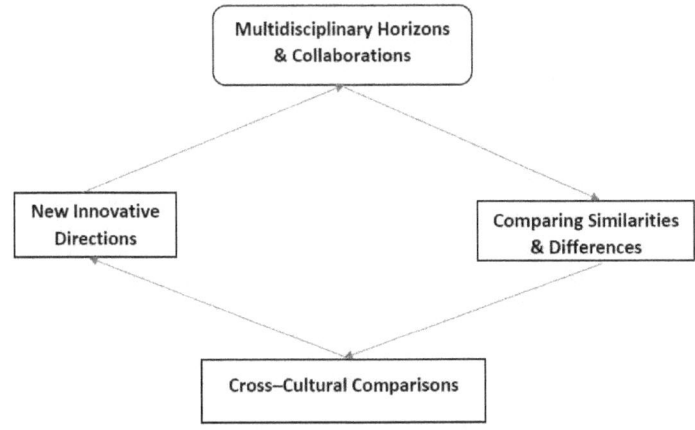

Figure 5.4: Fundamentals of multidisciplinary horizons.

1. Multidisciplinary Horizons and Collaborations lead you to **compare similarities and differences** in themes that two or more disciplines analyze.

    While writing a research paper on modeling human emotions with my colleague from Riga Technical University Department of Artificial Intelligence, I focused on the mathematical traits while she focused on the programming characteristics.

2. Multidisciplinary horizons and collaborations direct you to **decipher cross-cultural comparisons** when studying different cultures.

    My students and I compared the similarities and differences between the American and Ukrainian economic systems and cultures while teaching my online course on "Introduction to Business Start-Ups" at the Academician Yuriy Bugay International & Scientific Technical University in Kiev, Ukraine.

3. Multidisciplinary horizons and collaborations guide you to **new innovative directions**.

My colleagues from Riga Technical University Department of Engineering Economics & Management recommended me to design and teach a hands-on multidisciplinary "Risk Management Seminar".

You expand your multidisciplinary and international horizons while you develop and teach courses and seminars outside your discipline. The next four sections will share about the specific discoveries of multidisciplinary horizons.

5.1 Introduction to Photography

I was invited to teach introduction to photography during my spring 2016 sabbatical at Liepaja University in Latvia. This was an honor for me as photography has been my hobby for more than 20 years. In fact, this is something that I wanted to do for quite some time. To share with others how I capture and photographically describe nature's special and rare moments.

The course's objectives were to describe emotions without words only with light. In addition, the course's aims were to get students familiarized with using techniques such as aperture, shutter speed, film speed and which specific lenses to use. Furthermore, the course's intents are to gain intuition when overexposure and underexposure of light occurs, how to handle these problems and produce welcoming and quality photographs. The cognate diagram in Figure 5.5 outlines the primary course objectives.

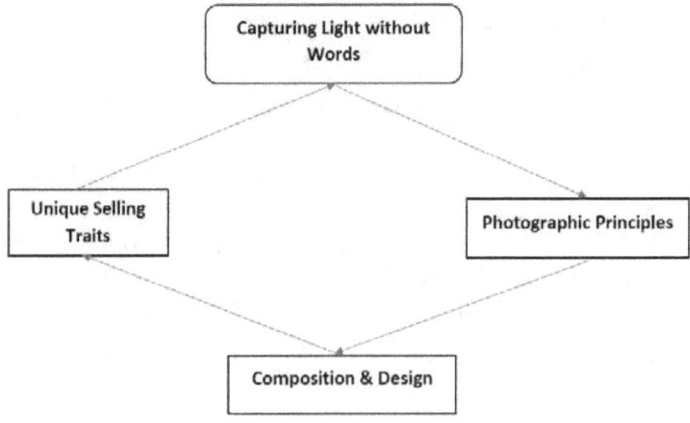

Figure 5.5: Fundamentals of introduction to photography.

1. Describing light without words lead you to the **principles of photography**. These include framing, rule of thirds, diagonal lines, and mergers.

2. **Principles of photography** then guide you to **composition and design**. These include four colors of natural sunlight, materials that reflect light, materials that absorb light, and materials that scatter light.

3. **Composition and design** then direct you to the **unique selling traits**. These include using photography to portray numerous moods, abstract and creative photography, and using additional welcoming photographic attributes.

I designed this as a hands-on course where starting with the second class, each student presented his/her photographs. First, to share about the motivation to capture the shot and then all the necessary photographic and technical details. Students could choose any theme for their photographs such as landscape, architecture, portraits, action shots, etc. Figure 5.6 presents a sample of a student's photograph taken in June 2018 (Gabriels Ziverts) rendering the green and red colors of a flower.

Figure 5.6: Green and red traits of a flower.

After each presentation, I would make comments and ask each student questions. I also offered other students opportunities to make comments and ask questions as well. Not only students gained photographic knowledge, but also gained experience in participating in discussions, asking questions and providing constructive feedback. This practice also exposed students to collaborative learning.

5.2 International Research Coalitions

After several years of international experiences with participating in several international conferences, international and multidisciplinary research projects and after developing and teaching courses and seminars, I decided to design a new seminar on "Developing International and Interdisciplinary Research Coalitions".

First, I offered this idea to the doctoral school at Riga Technical University in Latvia and conducted this 2-day hands-on multidisciplinary seminar for doctoral students. The corresponding diagram in Figure 5.7 depicts the course's principle objectives.

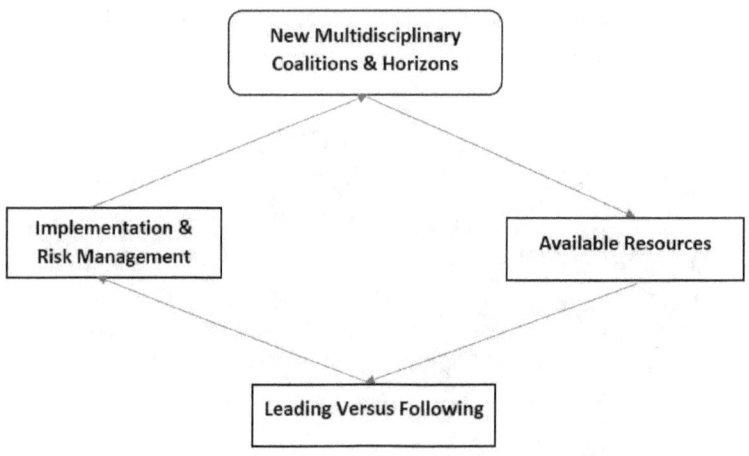

Figure 5.7: Principles of international research coalitions.

The first day of the seminar focused on developing international and multidisciplinary research coalitions by addressing the following questions:

1. Why establish interdisciplinary and international collaborations?
2. How to start interdisciplinary and international collaborations?
3. What are the available resources?
4. What are the good questions to ask?
5. Asking the right questions that may lead to collaborations?

The second day of the seminar focused on the implementation of the developed ideas by focusing on the corresponding questions:

1. Why implementations fail?
2. How to implement innovations effectively?
3. What is leadership and categories of leadership?
4. How leadership and innovation connect together?
4. Balance between leading and following?
6. Risk management and minimizing the risk of failure?

The students participated very actively by answering questions and shared about their experiences that were beneficial to other students and to me as well. Figure 5.8 presents the students' evaluations from the seminar conducted at Riga Technical University Doctoral School in June 2017.

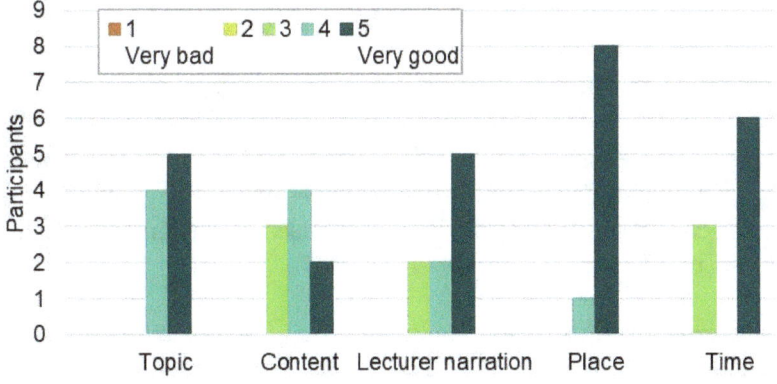

Figure 5.8: Students' seminar evaluations conducted in June 2017.

I had the opportunity to conduct this seminar in an online environment hosted by the EKA University of Applied Sciences in Riga, Latvia. More details addressing online teaching and learning will be discussed in Chapter 8.

5.3 Risk Management Seminar

My colleagues from Riga Technical University Department of Engineering Economics and Management asked me to conduct a "Risk Management Seminar" after we met at a conference. I then assembled this pilot multidisciplinary and applied hands-on seminar with various applications such as automobile and medical insurance rates, traffic safely, technical safety and fire safety. The associated diagram in Figure 5.9 describes the seminar's primary objectives.

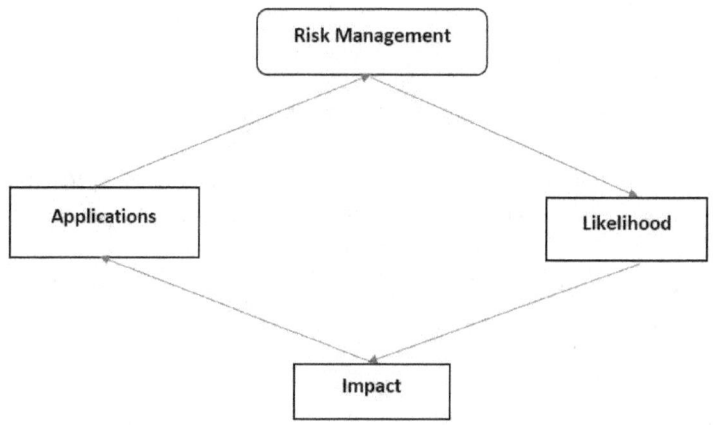

Figure 5.9: Fundamentals of risk management.

The seminar focused on the likelihood and impact, where the likelihood addressed the probability or chances and the impact addressed the consequences. In fact, the impact focused on the amount of financial and psychological damages such as:

1. The magnitude of damage to a vehicle or mechanism after an accident.

2. The magnitude of damage to an engineering structure after an accident.

3. The magnitude of damage after fire.
4. Severity of injuries and medical bills.

During each seminar, the participants and I compared the similarities and differences between the American and Latvian systems. For instance, we compared how the automobile insurance companies make a decision when to raise a driver's insurance.

In addition, I conducted a special version of the seminar that focused on applications of Risk Management in fire safety. Several staff from the Riga Fire Department joined such as dispatchers and fire fighters. They were very interested in the similarities and differences how the Riga Fire Department and the American fire departments operate.

I had the opportunity to conduct this seminar in an online environment. More details on the online teaching and learning will be discussed in Chapter 8.

5.4 Introduction to Business Start-Ups

On the base of my seminar "Developing International & Interdisciplinary Research Coalitions" that I conducted several times, I decided to develop a new hands-on multidisciplinary course on "Introduction to Business Start-Ups". The consequent diagram in Figure 5.10 presents the course's main principles.

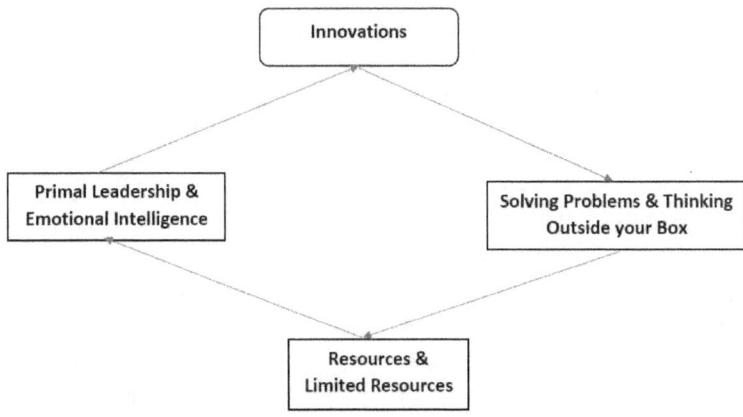

Figure 5.10: Principles of Business Start-Ups.

Figure 5.10 also focuses on the corresponding topics:

1. What is creativity and how it naturally emerges?
2. Flexibility to feedback and why feedback is crucial?
3. Uniqueness and benefits of a product?
4. What is primal leadership and emotional intelligence?
5. Thinking outside your comfort zone and asking the right questions?
6. Limited resources and functioning within limited resources.
7. Turning an innovation into reality.

The students participated actively by asking questions, answering questions and providing comments. I assigned the students weekly homework assignments. For instance, one homework assignment required students to pick a corporation which they liked and to describe its' specific strengths, winning strategies, unique marketing strategies, and discuss future suggestions for some improvements. In addition, I assigned students a course project which consisted of designing a potential business start-up. Each student gave a presentation on it during the last day of class. Furthermore, the students and I compared the similarities and differences between the American and the Ukrainian cultures, academic systems and economic systems.

This course was taught only in an online teaching and learning atmosphere. Students participated very actively by asking questions, answering questions, providing comments and sharing about their experiences. This course introduced students to experiential learning and collaborative learning.

5.5 Summary

Not only multidisciplinary horizons unfold perspectives to new collaborations such as new research projects, new courses and seminars but can also bridge two or more concepts, disciplines, and cultures together. The photograph in Figure 5.11 displays a railroad bridge in Riga, Latvia connecting the Old Riga and the Modern Riga.

Figure 5.11: Railroad bridge in Riga, Latvia.

More attributes of bridging two or more concepts, disciplines, and cultures together will be examined in Chapter 7.

5.6 Further Thoughts

1. In Section 5.1, we discussed the details of the hands-on course on "Introduction to Photography". Should I permit students to use cellular phone cameras and cameras from tablets? Do you think that these cameras will produce welcoming and selling photographs?

2. In Section 5.2, we discussed the design of the multidisciplinary hands-on seminar on "Developing International & Interdisciplinary Research Coalitions". How to make this course more accessible to undergraduate students and attract undergraduate students?

3. In Section 5.3, we discussed the attributes of "Risk Management Seminar". Should you offer this seminar to students outside the Department of Engineering Economics and Management?

4. In Section 5.4, we discussed the logistics of the multidisciplinary hands-on course on "Introduction to Business Start-Ups". How do you attract more students from non-STEM disciplines to take this course?

Chapter 6

Resources and Feedback

This chapter will focus on originating new courses and seminars in different academic systems together with the use of resources and feedback. This then directs you to asking the following questions: What are the available resources? How do you find available resources? Why limited resources arise? How do you function effectively and efficiently within limited resources? Why is feedback a resource? How do you apply feedback as a resource? The aerial photograph in Figure 6.1 asks the following question: What are the available natural resources on the Aegean Island.

Figure 6.1: Available resources on the Aegean Island?

Figure 6.1 then leads you to discovering available natural resources such as water and food which are essential for survival. This then directs you to asking the corresponding questions: How do you find these essential resources? Where do you find these essential resources?

6.1 Available Resources

Finding available resources for your course and seminar is the first vital step for expanding your international and multidisciplinary horizons and developing new courses and seminars. The succeeding diagram in Figure 6.2 decomposes available resources into primary resources and secondary resources that navigate you to successful outcomes.

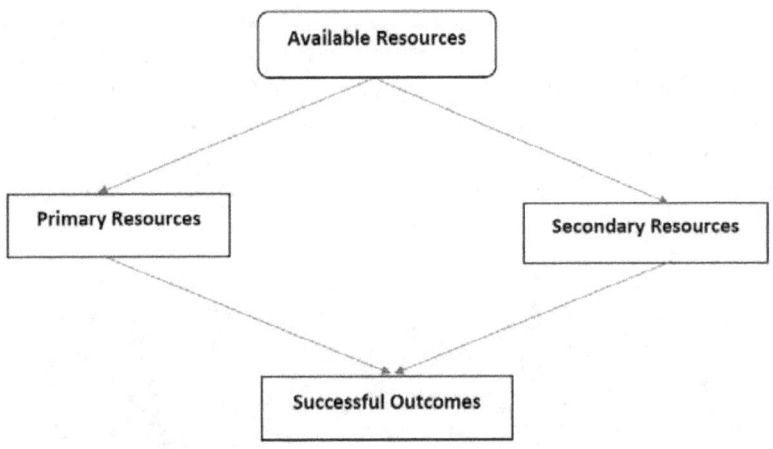

Figure 6.2: Primary and secondary resources.

1. First, **available resources** are **primary resources** in your new pilot project include time, money, support, and experiences and training. More attributes on Primary Resources will be discussed in Section 6.1.1.

2. **Available resources** also include **secondary resources** such as asking the right questions, noticing specific details and problems,

flexibility to feedback from colleagues and friends, critical thinking and non-standard approach to solving a specific problem. More attributes on Secondary Resources will be discussed in Sections 6.1.2 and 6.1.3.

3. **Primary Resources** and **Secondary Resources** then lead to **successful outcomes**. More attributes on Successful Outcomes will be discussed in Sections 6.1.1–6.1.3.

The next two Sections 6.1.1 and 6.1.2 will focus on the attributes of Primary and Secondary Resources and how they can navigate you to successful outcomes in your new international and multidisciplinary courses and seminars.

6.1.1 *Primary Resources*

Primary resources are transparent resources that you will frequently encounter. The marine landscape in Figure 6.3 paints a clear view of the available resources along the Baltic Sea shores in Latvia.

Figure 6.3: Resources along the Baltic Sea shores in Latvia?

Primary resources then address the following questions: How much interest do the administrators and students express for a new course? How much funding is available to conduct a seminar? How much experience does a professor have to conduct a new seminar?

The organizers at the University of Latvia and high school students approved my proposal for "Math Olympics in American Style" based upon the analogous competition "MATHBOWL" that I conducted at RIT. Sixteen school districts and close to 100 high school students throughout Latvia participated in this annual event. The organizers and students appreciated the challenging annual event that welcomed new international perspectives.

The Rezekne Technical Academy High School principal and high school students approved my course on "Introduction to Recognition and Deciphering of Patterns" as I taught Discrete Mathematics and Difference Equations at RIT and as I specialize on teaching university level mathematics to high school students. The high school principal and students gave me very supportive feedback and evaluations.

Liepaja University administrators and students approved my "Introduction to Photography Course" as photography has been my hobby for more than 20 years. The students appreciated the hands-on practice that the course offered and gained experiences in presenting their work and asking their classmates questions.

6.1.2 *Secondary Resources*

Secondary resources are more hidden resources in comparison to primary resources and navigate you to asking the right questions, to noticing supplemental details, thinking outside your comfort zone and considering non-standard approaches to solving specific problems. More details on asking the right questions will be addressed in Section 6.1.3. The clouds and the snow in Figure 6.4 portray a mystic view of the available resources that can be quite challenging to find within the alpine terrain in Banff National Park, Canada.

Figure 6.4: Resources in the Canadian Rockies' alpine terrain?

Secondary resources address the following questions: What theme do you choose to ignite the administrators' and students' interest for a new courses? How do you convince the administrators and students that you have enough experience to conduct a specific seminar? How is your course or seminar unique in comparison to the existing ones? How will the students and participants benefit from your course or seminar? How will the experiential and collaborative learning be implemented?

Riga Technical University Doctoral School approved my seminar on "Developing International & Interdisciplinary Research Coalitions" after examining my proposed lesson plans that described the benefits that the seminar would offer to the students. I presented a welcoming story why building strong international and multidisciplinary relations will be very instrumental to the graduate students.

The administration at the Academician Yuriy Bugay International & Scientific Technical University approved my course on "Introduction to Business Start-Ups" after several meetings and revisions of my proposed course contents. I successfully convinced the university's administration how the course's themes and outcomes will be rewarding to the students and that such a course will expand the university's international reputation and open windows and doors to new international and multidisciplinary relations.

6.1.3 *Asking the Right Questions*

Asking the right questions helps you start observing specific problems and details that only you may see and to asking non-standard and non-traditional questions. Asking the right questions then invites you to finding non-standard solutions to peculiar problems and may also pilot you to welcoming windows and doors of new perspectives. Figure 6.5 traces an inviting seascape to the unique rainbow cloud formation along the Atlantic shores in Brigantine, New Jersey.

Figure 6.5: Rainbow cloud along the Atlantic shores of Brigantine, New Jersey.

Capturing the inciting rainbow-shaped cloud in Figure 6.5 then compels you to ask the cognate questions: What natural factors formed such a cloud in a determined rainbow shape? Perhaps this phenomena occurred due to the change of tides from high tide to low tide? Maybe this happened as the fog merged together with the rainbow? Could a specific ocean breeze possibly form such a cloud?

Asking the right questions also navigates you to the expansion of your international and multidisciplinary horizons as it will frequently force you to think beyond your experiences and intuitions. Figure 6.6 presents the foundations of asking the right questions that lead to the expansion of your horizons, experiences and intuitions.

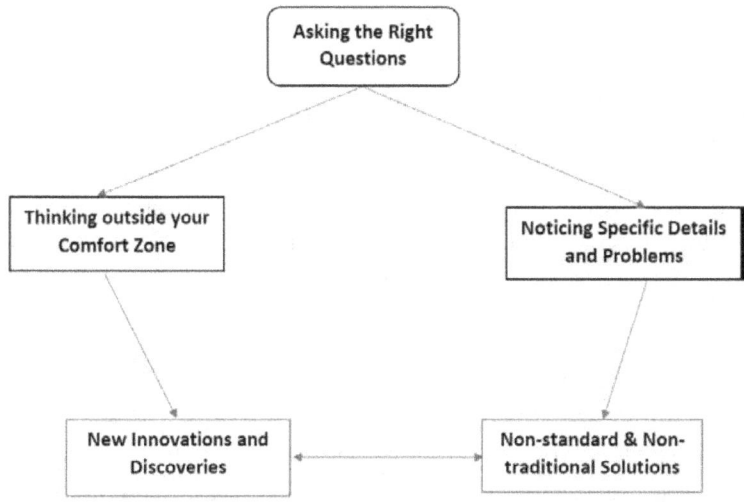

Figure 6.6: Asking the Right Questions Diagram.

1. First, **asking the right questions** coerces you to notice additional details, to think outside your comfort zone, which then navigates you to think beyond your experiences and intuitions.

    Teaching the "Introduction to Business Start-Ups" course provided me with new opportunities to compare the similarities and differences between the American and Ukrainian cultures, academic and economic systems. The students and I compared the two educational systems, value orientations and economic systems which then resulted in numerous robust discussions. It also welcomed my students to new themes such as categories of leadership, emotional intelligence and efficient use of limited resources and collaborative learning.

2. **Asking the right questions** persuades you to **notice specific details and problems** that few people may observe or only you may notice. This then prompts you to develop new and non-standard solutions.

While teaching Discrete Mathematics at RIT and at the Transportation and Sakaru Institute, I noticed that students experienced challenges with algebraic proofs and proof by induction method. To solve this problem and get students to be better with proofs, I provided more guided examples that emphasized how to interpret what they are asked to prove and indicated the specific vital algebra techniques to use during the process.

3. **Thinking outside your comfort zone** seeks you to **new innovations and discoveries** and also expands your international and multidisciplinary horizons.

    For me, participating and presenting at various international and interdisciplinary conferences taught me numerous principles about effective communication. In particular, through trial and error I learned effective communication with participants from various countries and disciplines. I then decided to expand my experiences by designing a seminar on "Developing International & Interdisciplinary Research Coalitions" with the aim to inspire students and participants to effectively develop their own international and multidisciplinary research coalitions.

4. **Noticing specific details and problems** opens windows and doors of new outlooks that can often steer you to new **non-standard and non-traditional solutions**.

    Encountering students' challenges with sequences directed me to develop a course on "Introduction to Recognition & Deciphering of Patterns" for high school students. This course provides students repetitive-type practice problems in detecting specific patterns and their applications. These practice problems then navigate students to solving recursive sequences, formulating patterns inductively and proving them. This style familiarizes and prepares high school students for university level mathematics.

6.2 Alternative Resources

Alternative resources often naturally emerge when desired resources become unavailable or when there are no available resources at all. From a distance, Figure 6.7 illustrates multiple paths to the highest pyramid-shaped peak.

Figure 6.7: Which path to take to reach the highest peak?

To determine which particular path you should hike will depend on the distance, the levels of difficulty, the wind direction and speed as well as your hiking experiences. It is not unlikely that you will hike more challenging alpine terrain if you choose the shorter hiking path in distance. Figure 6.8 describes the fundamentals of alternative resources.

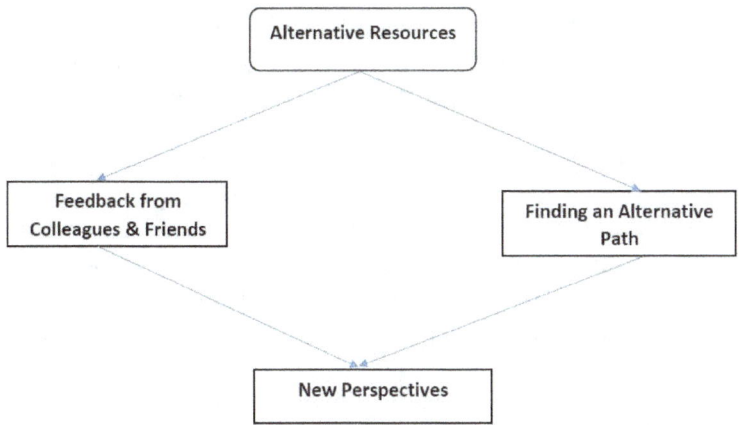

Figure 6.8: Alternative resources diagram.

1. **Alternative resources** can frequently emerge as **feedback from colleagues and friends**. Flexibility to feedback is vital as your colleagues and friends often see concrete details that you may not see or do not see. Your colleagues and friends may recommend you to design a new course or a course with a specific theme that you would never think of.

   My colleagues from Riga Technical University Department of Engineering Economics and Management recommended me to design a "Risk Management Seminar" for their students. My colleagues from the Rezekne Technical Academy High School asked me to teach a university level mathematics course for high school students.

2. An **alternative resource** can commonly be comprehended as an **alternative path**. When a given path from point A to point B is closed, you can generally find an alternative path. This situation can occur when you aim for a specific Resource A but your colleagues direct you to Resource B or C instead.

   During my spring 2016 sabbatical, I wanted to teach either Multi-variable Calculus or Complex Variables at the Transportation & Sakaru Institute in Riga, Latvia. On the other hand, my colleagues recommended me to teach a course on "Introduction to Discrete Mathematics for Electronic Engineers" instead.

   I wanted to expand on teaching my seminar on "Developing International & Interdisciplinary Research Coalitions" that I taught successfully at Riga Technical University, however my colleagues in Kiev advocated me to consider designing a course on "Introduction to Business Start-Ups" instead.

3. An **alternative path** and **feedback from colleagues and friends** guide you to windows and doors of new perspectives.

   Teaching Discrete Mathematics at RIT and at the Transportation & Sakaru Institute guided me to focus on recognition and formulation of patterns. This then directed me to new teaching practices and making mathematics accessible to students with different backgrounds and preparations.

   Teaching Introduction to Business Start-Ups in Kiev navigated me to discovering new international and multidisciplinary frontiers and to making international and multidisciplinary education accessible to everyone in the online environment.

The fundamentals illustrated in Figure 6.8 then guides you to the essentials of Feedback.

6.3 Feedback

Feedback can often provide one of the must crucial resources. Your students, colleagues and friends can be more experienced than you in certain disciplines and aspects and see specific details that you may not see or do not see. For instance, someone may recommend you to visit and discover the beauties and secrets of the Southern and Alpine Coast of Crete resembled in the corresponding photograph.

Figure 6.9: Southern and Alpine Coast of Crete.

Figure 6.9 greets the mystic Mediterranean-marine landscape with its' unique shades of green and blue and with its' unique alpine terrain. Analogous to Figure 6.9, feedback can often welcome new innovations such as new teaching practices, new courses, new seminars and new research directions, themes and collaborations.

Feedback is a vital resource as it is the first step in becoming a pedagogical leader and innovator. Another essential trait of a pedagogical leader and innovator is to carefully analyze students' feedback from the course evaluations (Herman, 2011). In fact, if several students write the same comment or similar comments, do they have good intentions to suggest future improvements in the course and in other courses (Smallbone & Quinton, 2010)? There are good reasons, especially if the same comment or similar comments appear on the evaluations during different semesters or during consecutive semesters (Hussain & Khan, 2016)? To retain amiable communication with the students and successful leadership, feedback is not only vital from students but is just as vital from colleagues. Figure 6.10 describes the essential characteristics of feedback.

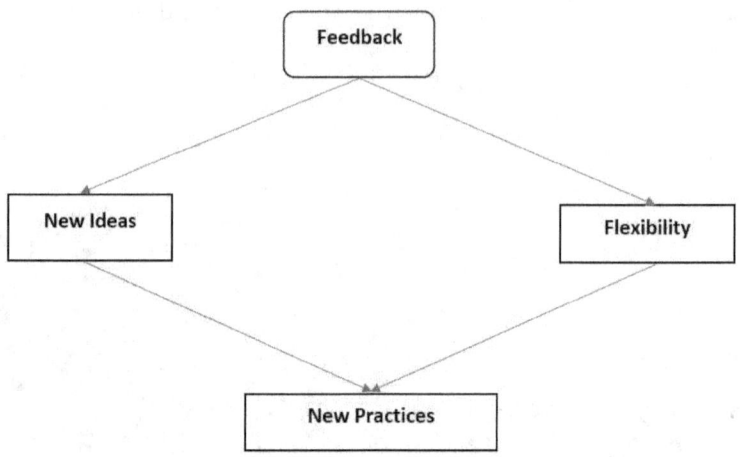

Figure 6.10: Essential characteristics of feedback.

1. First, **feedback** from students, colleagues and friends emphasizes weakness and areas of confusion. Furthermore, it introduces you to **new ideas** such as new teaching techniques and practices, and new research methods and directions.

    While teaching my online courses synchronously at RIT, several students recommended me to use the Zoom white board. This was very beneficial to me and the students as the Zoom white board has a numerous selection of colors and students can save each file in the jpg format directly from their computer screen. Not only students recommended me to use the Zoom white board but also guided me step by step on how to use it. Students asked more questions after I started to use it and I answered questions more efficiently while using the Zoom white board. Figure 6.11 portrays an example of the ratio test on the Zoom white board.

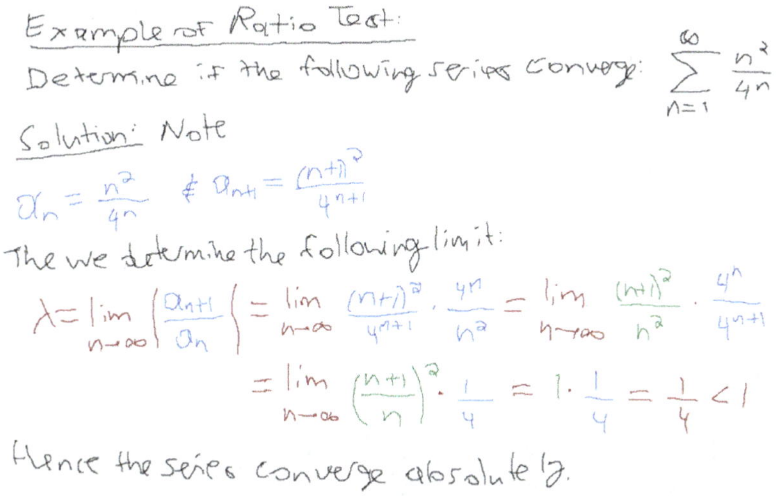

Example of Ratio Test:
Determine if the following series converge: $\sum_{n=1}^{\infty} \frac{n^2}{4^n}$

Solution: Note
$a_n = \frac{n^2}{4^n}$ & $a_{n+1} = \frac{(n+1)^2}{4^{n+1}}$

The we determine the following limit:
$$\lambda = \lim_{n \to \infty} \left| \frac{a_{n+1}}{a_n} \right| = \lim_{n \to \infty} \frac{(n+1)^2}{4^{n+1}} \cdot \frac{4^n}{n^2} = \lim_{n \to \infty} \frac{(n+1)^2}{n^2} \cdot \frac{4^n}{4^{n+1}}$$
$$= \lim_{n \to \infty} \left(\frac{n+1}{n}\right)^2 \cdot \frac{1}{4} = 1 \cdot \frac{1}{4} = \frac{1}{4} < 1$$

Hence the series converge absolutely.

Figure 6.11: Ratio test and the Zoom white board.

2. **Feedback** opens windows and doors to **flexibility**. It is important to be open minded to your colleagues' suggestions and constructive criticisms as they see certain details that you may not see.

    Several students suggested me to post the course notes right before class while teaching my online courses at RIT. This will provide students opportunities to follow the material posted in pdf format on their computer screens while I am teaching. In addition, several students recommended me the post the pdf files from which the videos were designed. These were very beneficial recommendations that enhanced the learning process for the students.

3. **New ideas** and **flexibility** then navigate you to **new practices**. These include new teaching practices and new research methods.

    The students repeatedly recommended me to include hands-on practice problems during class time in my upper level courses that I teach at RIT. In courses such as Multi-variable Calculus and Introduction to Complex Variables. To implement the students' recommendations, I decided to let students try solving each example on their own instead of working out the details as I have done previously. I supervised the students' progress while they were working on each example and assisted them with their questions. Furthermore, I emphasized the students' common mistakes, indicated how to correct each mistake, set up each problem correctly and which essential steps must be shown.

6.4 Limited Resources

Limited resources frequently arise due to numerous factors beyond your control. These factors may include money, time, limited experiences, self confidence, risk, support and other factors. The succeeding photograph in Figure 6.12 provides an aerial example of the limited resources along the rugged Labrador coast.

Figure 6.12: Limited resources along the Labrador coast.

Note that the nordic landscape in Figure 6.12 appears barren from above due to limited natural resources as there is almost no vegetation and fresh water. In addition, harsh climatic circumstances in Figure 6.12 comprise limited resources. The challenging weather conditions also restrict activities such as hunting and fishing.

This section will address the following question: How do you function effectively within limited resources and maximize the outcomes? The consequent diagram in Figure 6.13 reveals some of the answers.

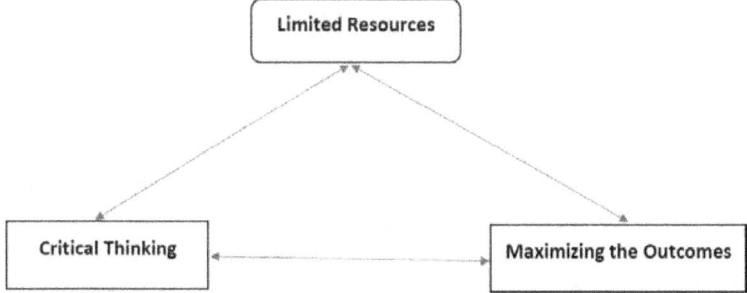

Figure 6.13: Functioning within limited resources.

1. **Limited resources** comprise common constraints such as time, money, limited experiences and support. Limited resources also raise the following questions: If you need 4 hours to conduct a seminar, how do you conduct it in 2 hours instead? Should you teach a course for the first time when you do not have enough experience? These questions will lead you to efficiency, prioritizing, sacrificing and to risk management.

    Academician Yuriy Bugay International & Scientific Technical University in Kiev, Ukraine asked me to give a presentation that outlines my course on "Introduction to Business Start-Ups". I was given 1-hour limit that also included time for questions and answers. I presented the unique traits of the course and how the students and the university will benefit from the course.

2. **Critical thinking** naturally emerges from **Limited resources**. Critical thinking will then steer you to alternative thinking and emotional intelligence.

    I could not include all the topics while teaching "Introduction to Math Olympics" for the first time as a pilot course. I then prioritized the most crucial topics as a fundamental base to pattern recognition to present to the students. These topics include linear patterns, geometric patterns, piecewise patterns, recursive patterns, proof by induction, properties of the Pascal's triangle and fundamentals of graph theory.

3. **Limited resources** will also navigate you to **maximizing the outcomes**, which you can interpret as the unique welcoming introduction, crucial knowledge, memorable course or seminar, etc.

At the international conference on Science, Education and Business in Modern Conditions hosted by the St. Petersburg State University of Economics in St. Petersburg, Russia, as one of the invited plenary speakers I had a 20-minute time limit to speak about online education. I chose to present the most essential characteristics of online education. These include effective communication, swift graded feedback, rapid exchange of information, flexible and amiable teaching and learning environment, functioning effectively in multiple time zones, and meeting and going beyond the expected learning outcomes.

6.5 Summary

The effective use of primary and secondary resources is a vivid path to reaching your destination. Figure 6.14 paints the snowy-white crests of the White mountains in New Hampshire as the enriching destination with a majestic mountainous view.

Figure 6.14: White mountains' snowy-white crests.

To reach the snowy zeniths in Figure 6.14 will require specific goals and experiences. It is essential to set your expected outcomes and outline your aims and experiences to reach your special gratifying destination. Furthermore, be ready to encounter challenges and obstacles and consider alternatives.

6.6 Further Thoughts

1. In Section 6.1.1, we discussed about experiences as vital resources to new teach a course or to conduct a new seminar. Will your abundant and diverse experiences guarantee approval for your new course or seminar?

2. In Section 6.1.2, we discussed about presenting a convincing argument for an approval. How do you design a unique and welcoming story to attract your new innovation?

3. In Section 6.1.3, we discussed about asking the right questions as a pertinent resource. What questions do you start asking your students, participants and colleagues to start a robust and memorable discussion?

Chapter 7

Promotion of Ideas and Innovations

This chapter will focus on the promotion of new ideas and innovations. How do you construct a unique welcoming story? How is your story unique and why should someone buy it? The succeeding photograph welcomes the eccentric Caribbean shores of Mexico.

Figure 7.1: The welcoming Caribbean Sea.

Figure 7.1 paints the Caribbean Sea with enchanting shades of green, blue and white together with the distinctive waves and clouds. In addition, Figure 7.1 describes the unique Caribbean characteristics. Why should you visit the Caribbean Sea instead of the Baltic Sea or the Aegean Sea? Identifying the unique selling traits of the Caribbean Sea first will help you sell your story, idea and innovation. What distinctive features you can only discover in the Caribbean Sea?

7.1 Evolving your Innovations

You build bridges between concepts, disciplines and cultures while developing your innovations. Evolving your innovation will guide you to gluing pieces of a specific puzzle by determining what two concepts, disciplines and cultures have in common and how they relate to each other. How do you bridge them together?

The upcoming two photographs illustrate the dark and mystic marine tornado cloud emerging on the horizon. The two photographs also paint shades of green and gray, solar paths navigating to the tornado cloud and bright solar rays burning through the tornado cloud.

The consequent photograph in Figure 7.2 paints a bright green solar path guiding to the dark and mystic Baltic tornado cloud along the shores of Latvia.

Figure 7.2: The dark and mystic Baltic tornado cloud.

The next photograph in Figure 7.3 resembles a bright silver solar path navigating to the dark and mystic Caribbean tornado cloud along the shores of Mexico.

Figure 7.3: The dark and mystic Caribbean tornado cloud.

First note the contrasting miens of the tornado cloud in Figures 7.2 and 7.3. The Baltic Sea in Figure 7.2 reflects the sunlight while the Caribbean Sea in Figure 7.3 absorbs the sunlight. Figure 7.2 traces a darker tone of gray in comparison to Figure 7.3. The green solar path leading to the tornado cloud gradually fades in Figure 7.2 in comparison to persistent bright silver path in Figure 7.3. The following diagram in Figure 7.4 outlines the fundamental attributes of developing innovations.

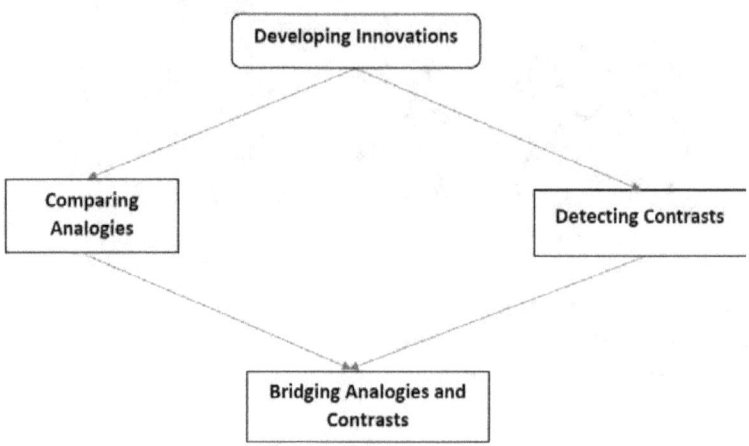

Figure 7.4: Fundamental attributes of developing innovations.

1. **Developing innovations** can include **comparing analogies**. This then steers you to recognize the similarities between concepts, disciplines and cultures. How do you perceive these similarities?

    While teaching my course on "Introduction Recognition & Deciphering of Patterns", I indicated the similarities between a system of diminishing equilateral triangles and a system of shrinking squares presented in the consequent two sketches in Figures 7.5 and 7.6.

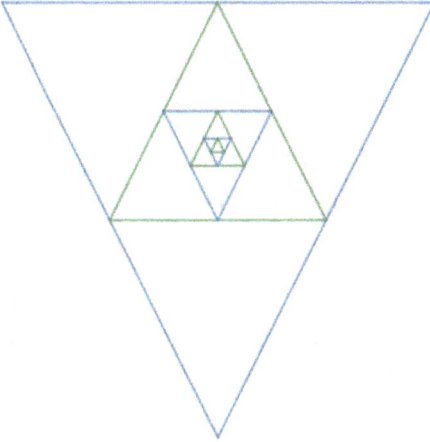

Figure 7.5: System of diminishing equilateral triangles.

Observe that Figure 7.5 sketches a system of diminishing equilateral triangles. Starting with the largest blue equilateral triangle, the sides of the neighboring green equilateral triangle meet at the mid-points of the largest blue equilateral triangle.

Figure 7.6: System of shrinking squares.

Analogous to Figure 7.5, Figure 7.6 describes a system of shrinking squares. Starting with the largest green square, the sides of the neighboring blue square meet at the mid-points of the largest green square.

2. **Developing innovations** will guide you to **detecting contrasts**. There are distinct contrasts between concepts, disciplines and cultures. How do you detect and utilize these distinct contrasts?

   The students and I focused on the contrasts between the American and Ukrainian economic systems, educational systems and cultures while I taught my course "Introduction to Business Start-Ups" at the Academician Yuriy Bugay International & Scientific Technical University in Kiev, Ukraine.

3. **Comparing analogies** and **detecting contrasts** should incline you to **bridging them together**. Connecting similarities and differences between concepts, disciplines and cultures expands your horizons and welcomes you to new perspectives.

   I emphasized the similarities and differences between a system of squares and a system of equilateral triangles as shown in the consequent two diagrams in Figures 7.7 and 7.8 while teaching my course on "Introduction Recognition & Deciphering of Patterns".

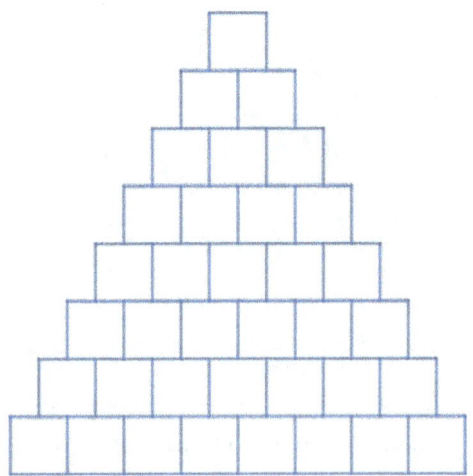

Figure 7.7: Pyramid-shaped system of squares.

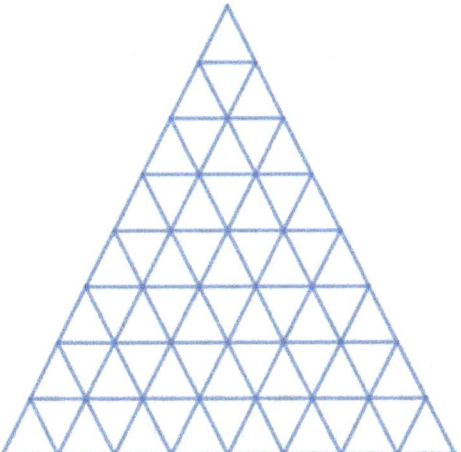

Figure 7.8: Pyramid-shaped system of equilateral triangles.

Figure 7.7 describes a system of squares with one square in the first row, two squares in the second row, three squares in the third row and so on. The total number of squares in Figure 7.7 is the corresponding sum of eight consecutive positive integers starting with 1:

$$1 + 2 + 3 + 4 + 5 + 6 + 7 + 8 = \sum_{i=1}^{8} i. \tag{7.1}$$

Similar to Figure 7.7, Figure 7.8 resembles a system of equilateral triangles with one triangle in the first row, three triangles in the second row, five triangles in the third row and so on. The total number of triangles in Figure 7.8 is the corresponding sum of eight consecutive positive odd integers starting with 1:

$$1 + 3 + 5 + 7 + 9 + 11 + 13 + 15 = \sum_{i=1}^{8} (2i - 1). \tag{7.2}$$

Observe that Figures 7.7 and 7.8 are both assembled with eight rows of squares and triangles. On one hand, via (7.1) we add eight consecutive integers to determine the total number of squares in

Figure 7.7. On the other hand, via (7.2) we add eight consecutive odd integers to determine the total number of triangles in Figure 7.8.

7.2 Revising your Innovations

Revisions of stories, ideas and innovations are essential as your initial draft will often have missing ingredients and as your colleagues and friends will see details that you may not think of. After observing and photographing numerous cloud systems and formations, by coincidence I noticed the following eruptive-shaped cloud system above the dunes along the Baltic Sea shores of Latvia that caught my eye.

It is therefore essential to be aware of minuscule details and be flexible to make any necessary revisions while designing your story, idea and innovation. You will seldom revise your initial draft only once. It may require several revisions. Your own horizons expand after each revision as you gain more insights. Figure 7.9 outlines the primary characteristics of revising innovations.

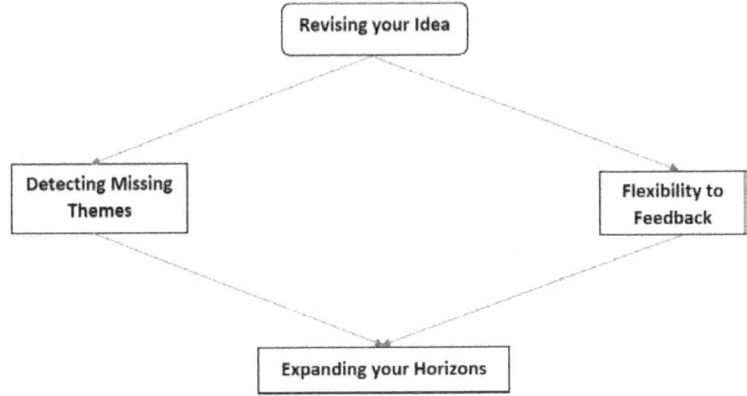

Figure 7.9: Primary characteristics of revising innovations.

1. **Revising your innovation** steers you to **detecting missing themes**. You will often discover missing themes after analyzing and proof-reading the initial draft of your idea.

    After conducting my seminar on "Establishing International & Interdisciplinary Research Coalitions" for the first time, I decided to include new themes such as risk management, outweighing the positives and negatives, primary and secondary resources and limited resources.

2. **Revising your innovation** also trains you to become more **flexible and open to feedback**. Your colleagues and friends will see specific themes and distinct details that you may not see.

    While designing my course on "Introduction to Business Start-Ups", my colleague from the Academician Yuriy Bugay International & Scientific Technical University in Kiev, Ukraine recommended me to add a lesson plan on "History of Technological Innovations".

3. **Detecting missing themes** and **flexibility to feedback** then **expand your horizons** as you see a broader picture.

    While revising my "Math Olympics in American Style Event", I first decided to balance the diversity of topics in the seven rounds of questions. Second of all, my colleagues from the University of Latvia Department of Mathematics recommended me to balance the difficulty level of questions from round to round and within each round.

7.3 Selling your Innovations

Assembling and selling your story, idea and innovation will convey your unique traits and direct you to asking the corresponding questions: What is unique about your innovation? How is your innovation different in comparison to the existing one? How is your innovation better than the existing ones? These questions will assemble your reflections in Figure 7.10 which outlines the principle attributes of functioning within limited resources.

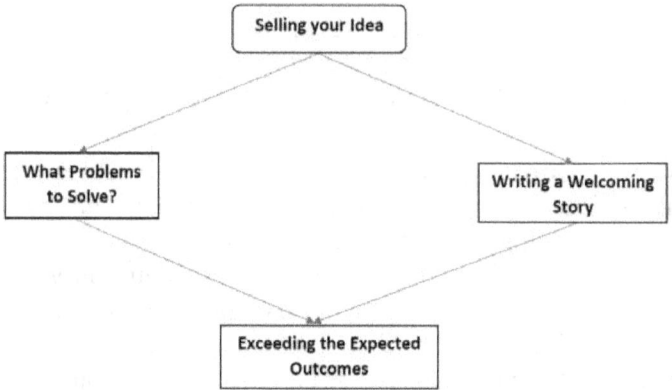

Figure 7.10: Functioning within limited resources.

1. **Selling your idea** pilots you to **writing a welcoming story**. Identify your attracting and unique features and enchanting traits. How do you convince someone to buy your story, idea or innovation?

    The selling traits of my course on "Introduction to Business Start-Ups" were that they welcomed new principles and provided numerous applied hand-on problems and cross-cultural comparisons. In addition, students enhanced their analytical skills, presentation skills, and collaborative learning.

2. **Selling your idea** then navigates you to **solving problems**. If you proclaim why certain problems exist and how to solve them creatively, you can then advocate how to solve them effectively and the welcoming benefits they bring. How do you persuade someone that distinct problems lead to destructive consequences? It is vital to determine the sources of the problems and to construct effective solutions to these problems.

My course on "Introduction to Recognition & Deciphering of Patterns" is designed to enhance students' algebra skills, analytical skills and programming skills while solving the assigned practice problems. Furthermore, students learn new problem solving techniques at the same time.

3. **Solving problems** and **writing a welcoming story** will lead to **exceeding the expected outcomes**.

   The digitized work-sheets with guided examples in my SAT Preparatory Course helped me achieve and exceed the expected outcomes. This saved time from writing on the white board and instead focus on solving numerous practice problems correctly and efficiently. Students received detailed feedback on how and why their mistakes emerged and how to correct them.

7.4 Summary

Designing a successful welcoming selling story is an essential trait that expands your intuitions, experiences, communication skills, critical thinking skills, problem solving skills and competitive skills. Figure 7.11 sketches a welcoming aqua-autumn scenery in Letchworth State Park, New York State.

Figure 7.11: Welcoming aqua-autumn scenery in Letchworth State Park.

Stimulating ideas and innovations will open new windows and doors of opportunities to international and multidisciplinary collaborations and to new courses and seminars in various academic systems.

7.5 Further Thoughts

1. In Section 7.1, we discussed comparing analogies and detecting contrasts while bridging two concepts, disciplines and cultures. Is it possible to bridge any two random concepts, disciplines and cultures? What challenges and barriers could emerge along the way?

2. In Section 7.2, we discussed detecting missing themes while revising your innovations. Why missing themes arise? How do you detect missing themes?

3. In Section 7.3, we discussed writing a welcoming story while selling your innovation. How do you design a welcoming theme to attract participants? Will the same welcoming story work in all learning environments?

Chapter 8

Online Teaching and Learning

Online education is the teaching and learning process that replaces the traditional classroom via computers and related technology. This is not a new practice but was forced upon all of us world wide during the 2020 pandemic. Distance learning officially commenced in the middle of the 19th century in the U.S. when the U.S. postal service was established. The practice of such distance courses started with the use of the postal service but involved long delays in the receiving of the material and graded homework assignments, essays and exams.

In 1873, the practice of distance learning transitioned to the development of "Society to Encourage Home Studies" in Boston, Massachusetts by Ana Eliot Ticknor.

Online Education efforts occurred outside the U.S. as well. In 1911, using the Australian Postal System, the Department of Correspondence Studies at the University of Queensland in Australia was established. In 1946, the University of South Africa became the champion and innovator of distance learning. With over 300,000 students, today the University of South Africa (Unisa) is Africa's largest open distance learning (ODL) institution (de Villiers & Queiros, 2016). Table 8.1 was designed by Ruth de Villiers and Dorothy Queiros presents the students' response rates to Video Clips and Web Sites in online courses at the University of South Africa.

Table 8.1: Items relating to video clips and web sites in 2016.

Item	Responses(%)					
	SD	D	U	A	SA	A & SA
1. The video clips helped me understand the application of the information better	5.0	5.0	34.0	39.0	17.0	56.0
2. Video clips helped the material come alive for me	3.4	6.8	40.7	32.1	17.0	49.1
3. Video clips helped me remember information better	6.8	5.1	40.7	25.4	22.0	47.4
4. The references to web sites enhanced my learning	1.7	8.5	15.2	47.5	27.6	75.1

Distance learning continued to progress with the use of television and the radio and then distance learning shifted to online education in the 1990's and widened its horizons parallel with the expansion of the digital era. In 1989 the University of Phoenix was the first university that opened its fully online bachelors and masters programs. Consequently, many other academic institutions have followed this practice.

Distance education expanded in Russia after signing the memorandum with UNESCO in 1997. Soon after, this led to the opening of MTI-VTU (Moscow Technical Institute-Global Technical University), which received accreditation in 2000 and continues to develop very actively. This institute offers numerous distance learning programs and issues diplomas. In 2005, distance learning expanded within the universities in the Russian Federation and in the training of personnel of large corporations such as the Russian Railways, SeverStal, and the Norilsk Nickel. In 2005, the Russian distance education programs were recognized on the international level by the International Association Advanced Distributed Learning (ADL).

This chapter's objectives are to explore the unique characteristics that the online teaching and learning environment offers. Today, these include introduction of new teaching innovations and practices and effective communication skills. Modern technology resolved many of the problems with time delays and offers swift and efficient interaction between professors and students. Hence the modern technology guides you to design an amiable and robust online teaching and learning atmosphere and to go beyond the expected learning outcomes.

The upcoming figures describe the motivations for online education. Figure 8.1 presents the students' factors in choosing online education programs.

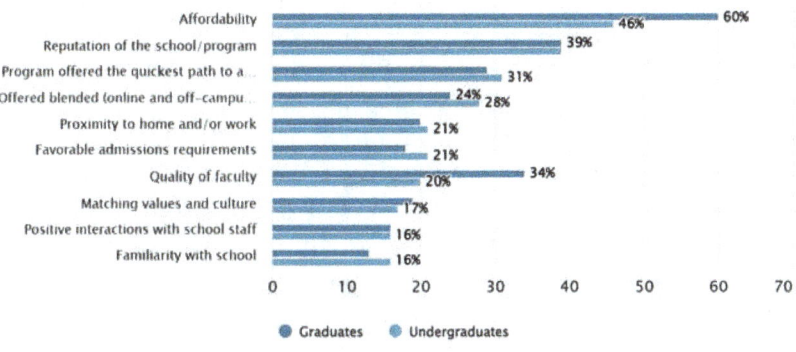

Figure 8.1: Online education-students' factors in 2020.

Figure 8.2 describes the categories of students who choose online education programs.

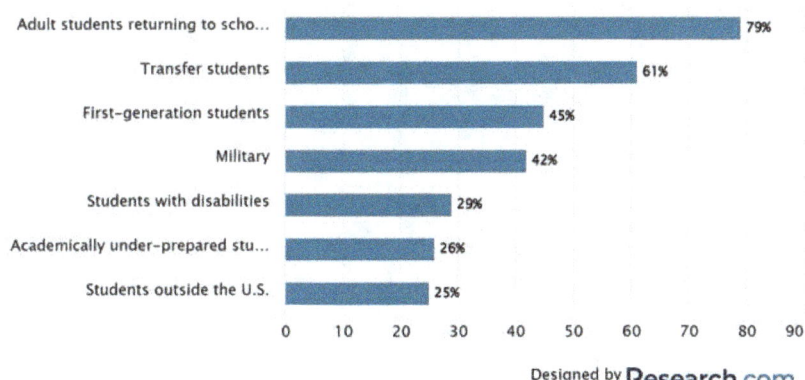

Figure 8.2: Online education-categories of students in 2020.

8.1 Successful Online Teaching Practices

The practice of online teaching and learning environments recently expanded since COVID-19 pandemic spread world wide as numerous universities and schools closed for quite some time. Online education continues to be an option at every school by necessity. This section's aims are to examine successful teaching practices in the traditional face-to-face and in online environments that navigate to reaching the expected learning outcomes.

The consequent two Sections 8.1.1 and 8.1.2 will focus on the following questions: Which teaching methods work for you in both environments? How do you transition from teaching in person within a classroom into an online atmosphere? What additional innovative techniques do you need to reach and perhaps go beyond the expected learning outcomes? Section 8.1.1 will analyze successful teaching techniques in mathematics courses and Section 8.1.2 in multidisciplinary courses.

8.1.1 *Online Mathematics Teaching Practices*

How do you design teaching strategies that invite a positive teaching and learning atmosphere either in the classroom, online or in a hybrid environment? Figure 8.3 outlines certain successful mathematics teaching tactics in the traditional face-to-face teaching and learning environment that progressed in the online teaching and learning environment.

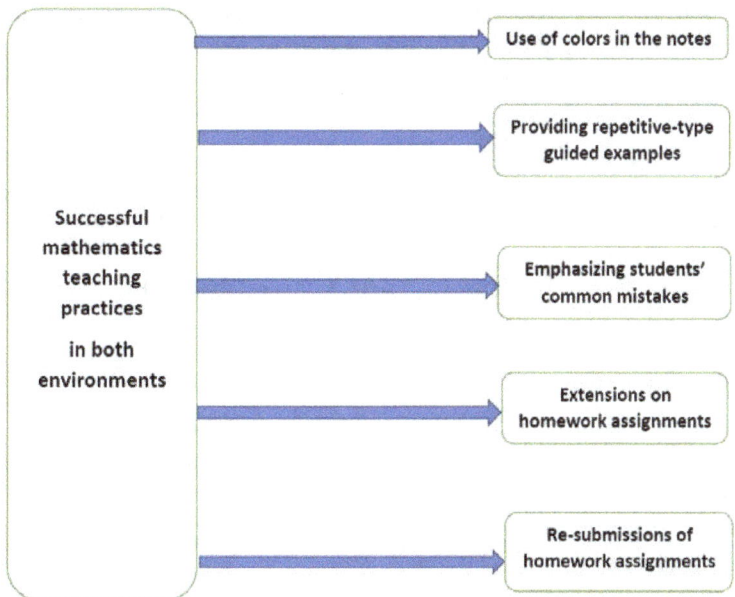

Figure 8.3: Mathematics online teaching tactics.

1. The use of different colors to decompose concepts into separate groupings is a successful teaching technique that I developed in my math courses. Particular groupings emphasize unlike patterns, specific integers, distinct families of functions, and vertices with different degrees.

Figure 8.4 traces an example of a semi-regular Lattice Graph $L_{2,5}$, where each vertex has degree either 2 or 3. The blue vertices V_1, V_5, V_6 and V_{10} have degree 2 while the green vertices V_2, V_3, V_4, V_7, V_8 and V_9 have degree 3.

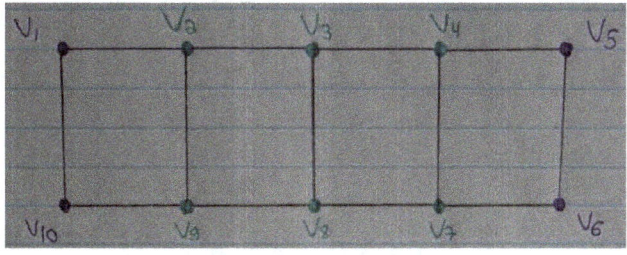

Figure 8.4: Semi-regular lattice graph $L_{2,5}$ with vertices of degree 2 or 3.

2. Providing repetitive-type guided examples with varying difficulty levels is another successful tactic that progressed in my math courses. These examples help students to gain grasp of certain concepts by solving numerous practice problems during class time and working on assigned homework problems.

   In my Introduction to Discrete Mathematics course, I invite students to verify the following **Integers' Identities**:

   2.1 Prove that the sum of three consecutive integers is divisible by 3.
   2.2 For $n \geq 1$, prove that the sum of $2n + 1$ consecutive integers is divisible by $2n + 1$.
   2.3 Prove that odd perfect squares are 1 more than a multiple of 8.
   2.4 For $k \geq 2$, prove that if there are $2k$ consecutive positive integers then at least $k + 1$ integers must be chosen to obtain at least one odd integer.

3. Indicating frequent mistakes that occur during practice problems in class and on homework assignments was mentioned in my students' evaluations quite many times. This tactic points out to students how and why specific mistakes occur and emphasizes how to apply certain techniques properly to solve related problems.

   In my Calculus II course, I emphasize the related common mistakes that I observe while grading their homework assignments related to trigonometric integrals:

   3.1 Incorrect use of trigonometric identities.
   3.2 Incorrect grouping of integrals.
   3.3 Incorrect use of Integration by Substitution.

4. Offering students extensions on homework assignments and multiple re-submissions of homework assignments successfully led to reaching the expected learning outcomes. Students gained the following advantages:

   4.1 To correct their mistakes.
   4.2 Get a stronger grasp of the concepts.
   4.3 To catch up with the course's schedule.

8.1.2 Multidisciplinary Online Teaching Practices

How do you create a dynamic teaching and learning atmosphere that steers you to achieving the expected learning outcomes in the online environment? Figure 8.5 traces specific thriving multidisciplinary strategies in the traditional face-to-face teaching and learning environment that enhanced in the online teaching and learning environment.

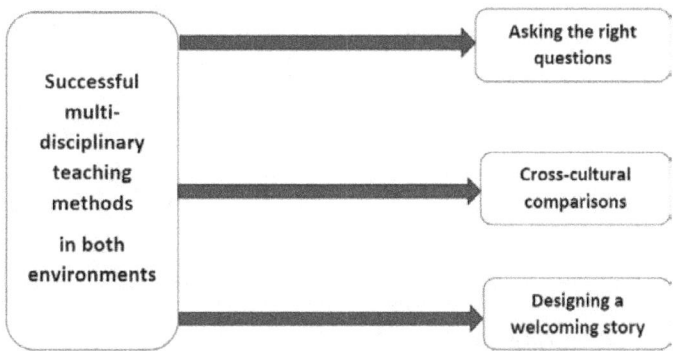

Figure 8.5: Multidisciplinary online teaching strategies.

1. **Asking the right questions** will ignite students' curiosities and stimulate robust discussions. It helps to direct the students' focus on distinct themes and to deeper questions to ponder about. Asking the right questions unfold new discoveries and challenges such as observing unusual details and finding non-standard solutions to certain problems.

    In my seminar on "Developing International & Interdisciplinary Research Coalitions" I welcome students to the following discussions: What questions do you ask speakers during a conference or a seminar presentation? What is the difference between good questions and right questions? How do you converse with a colleague from a different discipline and educational background and with different experiences at a multidisciplinary conference? When do you take the lead and when do you follow?

2. **Cross-cultural comparisons** open new windows and doors of opportunities to compare analogies and contrasts between different cultures. Cross-cultural comparisons widen students' analytical skills.

In my course on "Introduction to Business Start-Ups" I invite students to compare the American and Ukrainian educational systems and economic systems. The students are then assigned certain homework assignments to analyze how American and foreign corporations operate in Ukraine.

3. **Presenting a welcoming story** during the first class will ignite interest and anticipation for the classes to follow. This is your chance to outline the course's or seminar's attracting features and introduce it to your students. This will also address the following students' questions: Why should I take this course or seminar? What knowledge and experiences will I gain?

In my course on "Introduction to Recognition & Deciphering of Patterns" I present applications of various patterns in geometrical constructions. I also welcome students to experience new formulations of certain patterns and inductive reasoning.

8.2 Expected Learning Outcomes and Beyond

Every designated course has certain learning outcomes to achieve. How do you achieve these learning outcomes in an online atmosphere? Achieving the expected learning outcomes is one of the most vital factors for you and for your students. In order to achieve the planned outcomes you should seek to learn new techniques, widen your own experiences and enhance your leadership skills. Articulating these goals and outcomes will gear your students to asking the following questions: What new knowledge and experiences will I gain? How will I apply the new knowledge? Figure 8.6 will focus on the principles of reaching the expected learning outcomes.

Figure 8.6: Principles of reaching the expected learning outcomes.

1. Retaining the **balance between leading and following** is an essential factor that will help your students reach their expected learning outcomes and destination. It is important for you to take the lead and navigate your students to success. On the other hand, it is just as vital to let students take the lead at times and offer them chances to gain practical experiences in leading.

    It is not uncommon to discover students' innovative ideas in solving distinct problems when you let them take the lead. Balance between leading and following focuses on the following aspects: Teaching versus learning, asking questions versus answering questions, suggesting ideas versus listening to ideas and individualized learning versus collaborative learning.

    In my course on "Introduction to Discrete Mathematics" I offer students opportunities to take the lead by inviting students to solve certain problems during class time. I ask my students specific questions that guide them in the right direction to solutions and to designing their individualized learning path. In the meantime, I emphasize common mistakes and creative solutions that arise along the way.

2. Offering students **flexibility** is the next pertinent factor that will help your students reach their expected learning outcomes and destination. Keep in mind that students in an online teaching and learning environment learn at different rates, maybe working full time and raising a family. How do you offer students flexibility and yet reach the expected learning outcomes?

    In my online courses, students wrote supportive comments on the following criteria in their student evaluations that address flexibility: Allowing extensions on homework assignments, multiple re-submissions of homework assignments, asking questions on homework assignments during class time and asking questions by e-mail.

    Allowing extensions on homework assignments offers students additional chances to master the course material at their own pace and relieves them from additional deadlines to worry about. Allowing multiple re-submissions of homework assignments provides students supplemental practice to grasp the course material. Allowing students to ask questions on homework assignments during class time helps them notice deeper details that they may not necessarily understand initially. Allowing students to ask questions by e-mail provides them additional reinforcement of the concepts and supplemental assistance in between classes and increases the speed of communication.

8.3 Advantages of Online Environment

What are the advantages of an online environment compared to the traditional face-to-face environment? This navigates you to examine the following questions: Why teach online? Why take online courses? Why participate in online seminars and conferences? Figure 8.7 addresses the features of these questions and outlines the advantages of the online environment.

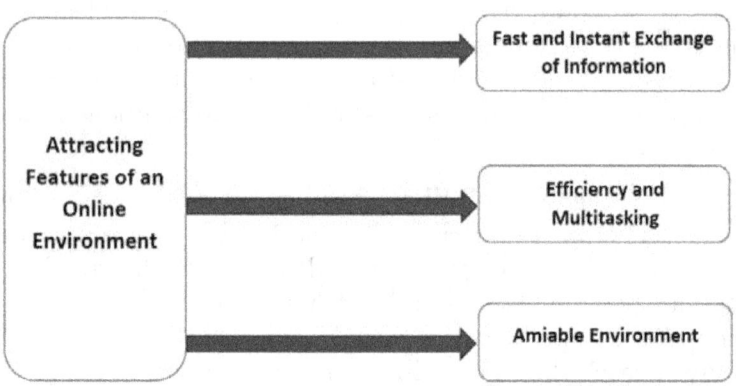

Figure 8.7: Advantages of online environment.

1. **Fast and instant exchange of information** is the first inviting feature of an online environment. Swift exchange of information during online lectures, seminars and conferences through the Zoom Chat and similar platforms. This includes:

    1.1 Swift exchange of contacts and publications during online seminars and conferences guided me in establishing future research collaborations.

1.2 Swift exchange of files and solutions during online lectures helps my students obtain a stronger grasp of certain concepts.

2. **Efficiency and multitasking** is the next welcoming characteristic of an online environment. This includes:

    2.1 The use of multiple files at the same time during online lectures to answer questions prepares my students in comparing similarities and differences between concepts.

    2.2 Multiple questions and comments through the Zoom Chat during online lectures, seminars and conferences steers me to investigate new research questions.

3. Swift exchange of information and multitasking design an amiable teaching and learning atmosphere. This includes:

    3.1 Swift graded feedback with written comments persuades my students to understand and correct their mistakes.

    3.2 The use of the Zoom white board and pdf files to ask and answer detailed questions motivates students to ask more specific questions related to class examples and homework problems.

    3.3 Answering questions by applying video platforms, different files, Zoom white board and e-mail stimulates students to understand the missing steps in the learning process.

The succeeding Sections 8.3.1 and 8.3.2 will examine deeper traits of Figure 8.7.

8.3.1 Why Teach and Take Online Courses?

What are the unique benefits of teaching online courses? What new and prosperous teaching techniques can you develop in an online environment? What are the benefits of taking online courses? What new learning skills can you and the students gain from an online environment? Figure 8.8 focuses on these questions and outlines the fundamental schemes.

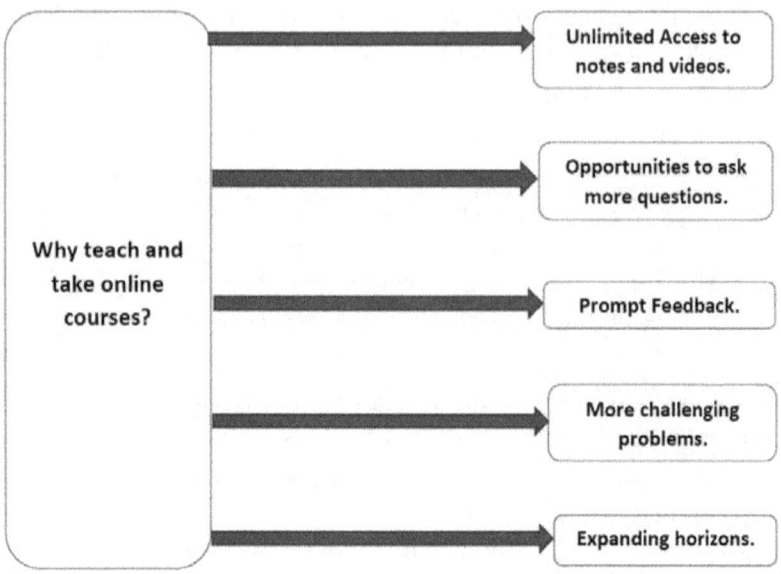

Figure 8.8: Scheme of teaching and taking online courses.

1. **Unlimited access to notes and videos** is a key selling feature of taking online courses. Your students can view the notes and watch the videos as many times as necessary at their convenience. This offers students opportunities to view the notes and videos in advance and learn the material on their own. This also offers slower students opportunities to catch up with the course material. Furthermore, if your students miss lectures then they have access to notes and videos at anytime.

2. **More opportunities to ask detailed questions** is both possible and easier for students who take online courses. From my experience in teaching online, there are more chances for students to speak up and ask questions. First, the students do not need to spend time copying notes and hence can concentrate on deeper details. As a consequence, this permits time during lectures to ask questions on the material as well as time at the end of each lecture to ask questions on homework assignments.

3. **Prompt feedback** certainly plays a crucial role in online courses. Prompt feedback with comments is an important navigation guide

for students to mastering concepts while enhancing their analytical skills. Instant graded feedback with comments is beneficial to your students as they can immediately catch their mistakes and understand how to correct them while the material is still fresh. Swift responses to questions by e-mail is also instrumental for your students as it steers them to identifying and correcting their mistakes.

In my "Introduction to Complex Variables" course, my students start to detect missing details in their proofs and solutions after they receive prompt answers to their questions by e-mail.

4. Online teaching provides an excellent opportunity for some students to solve **more challenging problems**. After receiving swift graded feedback with written comments, your students get additional chances to solve specific problems again and strengthen their intuitions. This practice leads them to understanding and solving more challenging problems.

In my "Calculus II" course, my students ask numerous questions on homework assignments and increase their comprehension of the concepts such as integration by trigonometric substitution, integration by parts and area in polar coordinates.

5. **Expansion of international and multidisciplinary horizons** is another appealing characteristic of online courses. An online teaching platform in American universities attracts more international students as many American universities offer internationally and multidisciplinary oriented programs of study. Recently this is also due to travel and financial restrictions.

My online courses that I teach at RIT attract foreign students from various countries such as United Arab Emirates, China and India. Foreign students especially take online courses offered during the summer sessions while they are have their summer internships. From my personal experiences, foreign students focus very carefully on specific details during lectures and in between lectures and direct their questions on these details and certainly enrich the international atmosphere in online courses.

Recently I developed and taught my online course on "Introduction to Business Start-Ups" at the Academician Yuriy Bugay International & Scientific Technical University in Kiev, Ukraine. I also designed and conducted my online seminar on "Developing

International & Interdisciplinary Research Coalitions" at EKA University of Applied Sciences in Riga, Latvia. In addition, I conceived and led the online "Risk Management Seminar" at Riga Technical University in Riga, Latvia.

8.3.2 Online Conferences

Online conferences welcome beneficial professional and new potential collaboration opportunities. What new research collaborations can you form? What new research directions can you consider? What new international and multidisciplinary research collaborations can you discover? Figure 8.9 addresses these questions and outlines the unique features and advantages of online conferences.

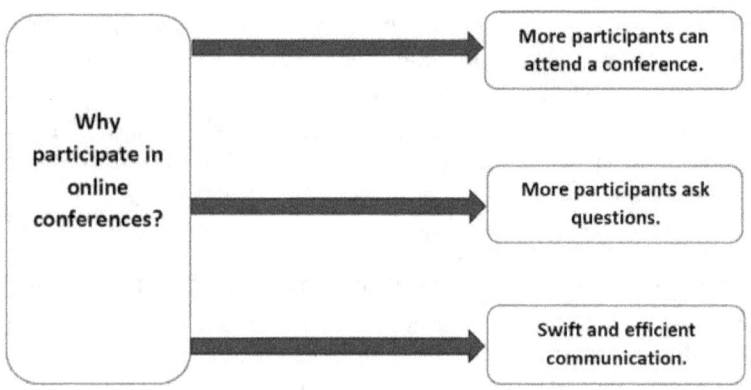

Figure 8.9: Characteristics of online conferences.

1. **Online conferences welcome more international participants** in comparison to attending the traditional face-to-face local and regional conferences. Scheduling and financial constraints can frequently limit international participants from attending certain conferences. In addition, limited available seating in some rooms may limit the number of participants in a special session. Participating in online conferences not only saves time and money, but also opens new windows and doors of international and multidisciplinary opportunities.

   In March 2021, I was invited to participate and present as one of the plenary speakers on "Bifurcations, Synchronization & Economic Cycles: Particularly in the Covid Era" at the

II International Scientific Conference on Finance and Financial Markets in the Context of Digitalization hosted online at RUDN University in Moscow, Russia.

2. **More participants ask questions during online conferences** in comparison to the traditional face-to-face conferences. Compact schedules and large amount of participants during face-to-face conferences can restrict and discourage participants from asking questions.

   In January 2021, I organized my special session on "Creative Teaching Methods That Lead To Student Learning" at the American Mathematical Society Annual Meeting 2021 hosted online in Washington D.C. I discovered that not only many more participants joined the session but also asked more questions in comparison to special sessions that I previously organized during traditional face-to-face conferences.

3. **Swift and efficient communication** is another inviting feature about online conferences. Large auditoriums and numerous scheduled back to back presentations in traditional face-to-face conferences often limit and delay the communication among the participants.

   During online conferences, exchange of information and contacts can be done very swiftly using Chats (on platforms such as Zoom, Google Meets, Microsoft Teams, etc.) at any time without causing any disruptions. Swift exchange of information then guides to more detailed questions and to new research directions and collaborations. The Chats also allow several participants to ask questions at the same time. Swift exchange of information keeps fresh outlooks on the current topics and agenda and can stimulate robust discussions.

8.4 Summary

The online teaching and learning environment opens new windows and doors of opportunities to new teaching practices, more efficient communication and international and multidisciplinary collaborations. Online teaching and learning environment also expands your intuitions, experiences, communication skills, critical thinking skills, problem solving skills and competitive skills.

8.5 Further Thoughts

1. In Section 8.1.2, we discussed about asking the right questions to stimulate a robust discussion. Will this technique always work in all the disciplines and cultures? What challenges and barriers could emerge along the way?

2. In Section 8.3.1, we discussed the advantages of teaching and taking online courses. How do you encourage more students to take online courses? How do you encourage more faculty to teach online courses? How do you break the phobias and misconceptions about online education?

3. In Section 8.3.2, we discussed the advantages of participating in online conferences. As a conference or a session organizer, what first question do you ask to generate more stimulating questions? The first question is the most critical question.

4. What are the disadvantages of online teaching and learning?

Chapter 9

Post Pandemic Environment

The corona virus pandemic in 2020 forced students, professors and many professionals to switch to working in an online environment. This was not a choice and was not an easy task for many. When the online teaching, learning and working environments expanded significantly with the corona virus pandemic, then the professors' and students' workloads increased from elementary school education through graduate school education levels. Did you look at the circumstance where the glass is half empty or half full? What new windows and doors of opportunities does it welcome for you? What new international frontiers emerge? The succeeding photograph welcomes the mystic alpine landscape of the Colorado Rockies and welcomes the new snowy alpine frontiers to discover that are beyond the tree line in higher altitudes.

Figure 9.1 addresses the answers to the questions and then guides you to the succeeding sections.

Figure 9.1: New post pandemic opportunities.

9.1 New Technologies and Applications

The necessary expansion of the online teaching, learning and working environments required using several new technologies and their applications. These include platforms such as Zoom, Microsoft Teams, Blue Jeans, Google Meets, Skype, etc. These platforms are used to conduct conferences, business meetings, seminars and to teach courses. Greenberg defines the online teaching and learning practice as a "planned teaching/learning experience that uses a wide range of technologies for distance learning and encouraging students" (Greenberg, 1998). In particular, the current computer technologies with various video platforms present new opportunities to conduct online communication in the synchronous and interactive style (Garlinska et al., 2021).

The synchronous style of online communication welcomes opportunities not only to ask questions but to receive instant answers in comparison to delays and limited communication that occur in the asynchronous style. Participants during online meetings, conferences and seminars can ask questions as in the traditional face-to-face environment. Note that participants can address their questions either verbally and by writing their questions by using the platform's Chat system. In addition, multiple participants can ask questions at the same time using the Chat system.

Students during online lectures can ask their questions directly either verbally, by using the Zoom Chat, by sharing a specific file and by using the electronic white board. This offers students further options to ask more detailed questions from which other students can benefit as well. These new tactics increase the efficiency in the communication between the students and the professor. Files can be transferred via Chat system and the work on the electronic Zoom white board can be saved as a jpg file. As a result, this refrains students from copying the work and instead concentrate on understanding the necessary details and concepts in greater depth.

9.2 New International Frontiers

The growth of the online teaching, learning and working environments also welcomes new international frontiers. The evolution of new international horizons in the online environment welcomes more foreign students from different countries taking online courses in American universities. This practice offers foreign students opportunities to study in a different academic system in the modern world with numerous travel, visa and financial restrictions. As we welcome more foreign students we analogously welcome American students and faculty members to new cross-cultural experiences. This presents collaborative learning and offers opportunities to learn from one another and to adapt smoothly to our new international environment. Foreign students ask different questions in comparison to American students as foreign students have different educational backgrounds, experiences and preparation levels. Online courses not only retain but enhance the diverse and international atmospheres in American universities. It offers a two-directional exchange between different cultures and academic systems. Figure 9.2 presents how many international students study in different countries.

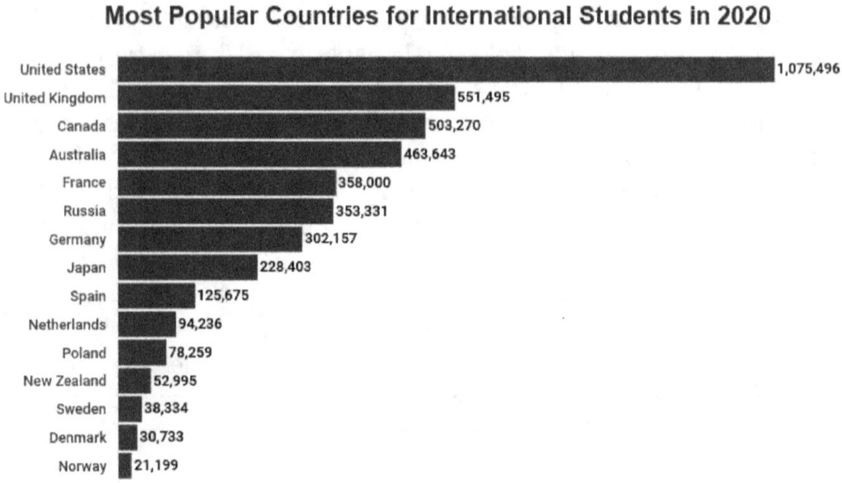

Most Popular Countries for International Students in 2020

Country	Students
United States	1,075,496
United Kingdom	551,495
Canada	503,270
Australia	463,643
France	358,000
Russia	353,331
Germany	302,157
Japan	228,403
Spain	125,675
Netherlands	94,236
Poland	78,259
New Zealand	52,995
Sweden	38,334
Denmark	30,733
Norway	21,199

Figure 9.2: Where international students study.

The practice of online seminars and conferences also stretches the international frontiers. Due to travel, visa and financial restrictions, this practice offers more opportunities for participants to attend more seminars and conferences. Participating in online seminars and conferences saves time and money. Participating in online seminars and conferences extends the international networking boundaries and welcomes new research collaborations. Online seminars and conferences increase the speed of communication and broaden the technological knowledge by applying new softwares and platforms.

9.3 Summary

The online teaching, learning and working environment opens new windows and doors of opportunities to expand efficiency, technologically, and internationally. During the corona virus pandemic, you transitioned from the traditional face-to-face environment to an online environment. When and how can you transition back to the traditional face-to-face environment? Will this be a smoother transition or a more challenging transition? What new techniques that you learned in the online environment can you reuse during the transition to the face-to-face environment? What new practices can you develop during the transition on the base of the successful strategies in the online environment?

9.4 Further Thoughts

1. In Section 9.1, we discussed about the technological advances as the corona virus pandemic arose in 2020. How do you make these distinct technologies available to everyone? How quickly can you master the new introduced technologies? How far will these technologies expand and how quickly?
2. In Section 9.2, we discussed the expansion of international frontiers as the online environment develops. What specific cultural barriers can emerge in the international online environment but not necessarily in the international face-to-face environment? How does the online environment limit the growth of international frontiers?

Chapter 10
Appendix

10.1 Developed Courses and Seminars

- Introduction to Difference Equations.
- Introduction to Research in Difference Equations.
- Applications of Difference Equation in Robotics.
- Introduction to Recognition and Deciphering of Patterns.
- Introduction to Math Olympics.
- Introduction to Photography.
- Introduction to Business Start-Ups.
- Writing a Welcoming Selling Story.
- Risk Management Seminar.
- Developing International and Interdisciplinary Research Coalitions.

10.2 International Collaborations

- University of Latvia, Riga, Latvia.
- Riga Technical University, Riga, Latvia.
- University of Liepaja, Liepaja, Latvia.
- Rezekne Technical University, Rezekne, Latvia.
- Transportation and Sakaru Institute, Riga, Latvia. Please add this after Rezekne Technical University.
- St. Petersburg State University of Economics, St. Petersburg, Russia.
- RUDN University, Moscow, Russia.
- Yaroslavl State University, Yaroslavl, Russia.

- Academician Yuriy Bugay International & Scientific Technical University, Kiev, Ukraine.
- Jagiellonian University, Krakow, Poland.
- Krakow University of Economics, Krakow, Poland.
- University of Foggia, Foggia, Italy.

10.3 International Workshops and Events

Workshop on balance between leading and following and international pedagogical innovations (conducted a special 1.5 hour workshop). Society, integration, education international scientific conference, Rezekne Academy of Technologies, Rezekne, Latvia, May 24–25, 2019.

Workshop on communication with the students outside the classroom & international teaching and learning (conducted a special 1.5 hour workshop). Society, integration, education international scientific conference, Rezekne Academy of Technologies, Rezekne, Latvia, May 25–26, 2018.

Math Olympics in American Style. Assembled seven rounds of questions, where each round has 12 questions. Close to 96 students from 16 different school districts throughout Latvia participated in this annual event. The University of Latvia Department of Mathematics hosted and sponsored this annual event.

10.4 International Conferences

The critical factors to innovation and Business Start-Ups. 10th International Scientific Practical Conference "Trade Marketing", ISMA University, Riga, Latvia, December 9, 2021.

New journey to discoveries in online teaching and learning; opportunities, innovations and challenges. International Conference on Science, Education and Business in Modern Conditions, November 26, 2021, St. Petersburg State University of Economics, St. Petersburg, Russia.

New journey to discoveries in online teaching and learning; opportunities, innovations and challenges. IV International Scientific Congress Society of Ambient Intelligence 2021, April 12, 2021, Krivoy Rog, Ukraine.

Bifurcations, synchronization and economic cycles: Particularly in the Covid era. II International Scientific Conference on Finance and Financial Markets in the Context of Digitalization (FFMD 2021), March 4, 2021, RUDN University, Moscow, Russia.

How to function efficiently within limited resources? How to utilize the resources efficiently? 8th International Scientific Conference on Sustainability in Energy and Environmental Science, October 21–22, 2020, Ivano–Frankovsk, Ukraine.

Value orientations, emotional intelligence and international pedagogical innovations and practices. 14th International Conference on Mathematics: Teaching, Theory & Applications; Athens, Greece, June 29–30, 2020.

Value orientations, emotional intelligence and international pedagogical innovations and practices. Society, Integration, Education International Scientific Conference, Rezekne Academy of Technologies, Rezekne, Latvia, May 22–25, 2020.

Efficient pedagogical management and leadership as a road to successful international teaching. Society, Integration, Education International Scientific Conference, Rezekne Academy of Technologies, Rezekne, Latvia, May 24–25, 2019.

Efficient pedagogical management and leadership as a road to successful international teaching. International Scientific Symposium "Economics, Business & Finance", July 10–12, 2018, Jurmala, Latvia.

Efficient pedagogical management and leadership as a road to successful international teaching. 5th International Scientific Conference New Trends in Management and Production Engineering Regional, Cross-Border and Global Perspectives; June 7–8, 2018, Brenna, Poland.

University level teaching styles with high school students and international teaching and learning. Society, Integration, Education International Scientific Conference, Rezekne Academy of Technologies, Rezekne, Latvia, May 25–26, 2018.

Communication with the students outside the classroom and international education. Actual Problems of Education (MIP 2017) TSI (Transportation and Telecommunications Institute); Riga, Latvia; June 1–2, 2017.

Communication with the students outside the classroom and international education. International Conference on Lifelong Education and Leadership; Liepaja University, Liepaja, Latvia; July 22, 2016.

Bibliography

Asmar, C., Baik, C., Naylor, R., & Watty, K. Good Feedback Practices-Prompts and guidelines for reviewing and enhancing feedback for students. Centre for the Study of Higher Education, The University of Melbourne, 2014.

Briere, D.E., Macsuga Gage, A.S., & Simonsen B. Effective teaching practices that promote a positive class environment. *Beyond Behavior*, 22(1) 2012, 14–22.

Brown, M.R. A pragmatic approach to the teaching of values. *Educational Horizons*, 36(3) 1958, 137–139.

de Villiers, M.R. & Queiros, D.R. Online learning in a South African higher education institution: Determining the right connections for the student. *International Review of Research in Open and Distributed Learning*, 17(5) 2016, 165–185.

Ekwueme, C.O., Ekon, E.E. & Ezenwa–Nebife, D.C. The impact of hands-on-approach on student academic performance in basic science and mathematics. *Higher Education Studies*, 5(6) 2015, 47–51, ISSN 1925–4741, E-ISSN 1925-475X.

Finch, D. & Jacobs, K. Online Education: Best practices to promote learning. *Proceedings of the Human Factors and Ergonomics*, 2012 56th Annual Meeting.

Garlinska, M., Masztalerz, K., Osial, M.A. & Pregowska, A. Worldwide journey through distance education–from the post office to virtual, augmented and mixed realities, and education during the COVID-19 pandemic. *Education Sciences*, 11(3) 2021, 118. DOI: https://doi.org/10.3390/educsci11030118.

Goodlad, J.I. Innovations in education. *The Educational Forum*, 31(3) 1967, 275–284.

Grasha, A.F. & Yangarber-Hicks, N. Integrating teaching styles and learning styles with Instructional Technology. *College Teaching*, 8(1) 2000, 2–11.

Greenberg, G. Distance education technologies: Best practices for K-12 settings. *IEEE Technology and Society Magazine*, (Winter) 1998, 36–40.

Hake, R.R. Interactive-engagement vs. traditional methods: A six-thousand-student survey of mechanics test data for introductory physics courses. *American Journal of Physics*, 66(1) 1998, 64–74.

Herman, R.L. What makes an excellent professor? *The Journal of Effective Teaching*, 11(1) 2011, 1–5.

Huberman, M. The role of teacher education in the improvement of educational practice: A linkage model. *European Journal of Teacher Education*, 6(1) 1983, 17–29.

Hunkins, F.P. & Ornstein A.C. Curriculum innovation and implementation. *Education and Urban Society*, 22(1) 1989, 105–114.

Hussain, M. & Khan, S. Students' feedback: An effective tool in teachers' evaluation system. *International Journal of Applied Basic Medical Research*, 6(3) 2016, 178–181.

Iyer, G., Tversky, B. & Zacks, J. Perceiving, remembering, and communicating structure in events. *Journal of Experimental Psychology: General*, 130(1) 2001, 29–58.

Keane, M. On retrieving analogues when solving problems. *The Quarterly Journal of Experimental Psychology Section A — Human Experimental Psychology*, 39(1) 1987, 29–41.

Kingsley Osueke K. & Kurt, S. *The Effects of Color on the Moods of College Students.* SAGE, 2014, 1–12

Maslakova, E.S. History of the development of distance learning in Russia. Text: Direct Theory and practice of education in the modern world: Materials of the VIII International Scientific Conference, St. Petersburg, Russia, St. Petersburg Publishing House, 2015, 29–32. URL: https://moluch.ru/conf/ped/archive/185/9249/.

Murgulis, E. Music repetition detection across multiple exposures. *Music Perception*, 29(4) 2012, 377–385.

Orlova, O. & Radin, M. University level teaching styles with high school students and international teaching and learning. *International Scientific Conference "Society, Integration, Education"*, 2018.

Orlova, O. & Radin, M. Balance between leading and following and international pedagogical innovations. *International Scientific Conference "Society, Integration, Education"*, 2019.

Radin, M., Riashchenko, V. Effective Pedagogical Management as a road to successful international teaching and learning. *Forum Scientiae Oeconomia*, 5(4) 2017, 71–84.

Radin, M. & Shlat, N. Value orientations, emotional intelligence and international pedagogical innovations. *The proceedings of the 7th International Scientific Conference "Society, Integration, Education"*, 2020, III, 732–742. DOI: http://dx.doi.org/10.17770/sie2020vol2.4858.

Radin, M. & Schlat, N. Online Education: Learning outcome, success & challenges. *The Proceedings of the International Scientific Conference "Society, Integration, Education"*, 1, 2021, 524–536. DOI: http://dx.doi.org/10.17770/sie2020vol2.4858.

Shields, P.M. A pragmatic teaching philosophy. *Journal of Public Affairs Education*, 9(1) 2003, 7–12.

Smallbone, T. & Quinton, S. Feeding forward: Using feedback to promote student reflection and learning — a teaching model. *Journal of Innovations in Education and Teaching International*, 47(1) 2010, 125–135.

Spendlove, M. Competencies for effective leadership in higher education, *International Journal of Educational Management*, 21(5) 2007, 407–417.

Stylianides, A.G. & Stylianides, G.G. Seeking research-grounded solutions to problems of practice: Classroom-based interventions in mathematics education. *ZDM–Mathematics Education*, 45(3) 2013, 333–341.

Venalainen, P. Contemporary art as a learning experience, Elsevier Procedia. *Social and Behavioral Sciences*, 45 2012, 457–465.

Von Glaserfeld, E. Cognition, construction of knowledge, and teaching. *Synthese*, 80(1) 1989, 121–140.

Yakovlev, Y. & Yakovleva, N. Interactive teaching methods in contemporary higher education. *Pacific Science Review*, 16(2) 2014, 75–80. DOI: 10.1016/J.PSCR.2014.08.016.

Index

A

academic innovations, 12
academic reforms, 27
academic system, 5, 61, 84
Academician Yuriy Bugay International & Scientific Technical University in Kiev, Ukraine, 55, 110
administration's final approval, 58
administration's interest in the topic or convincing the administration, 57
Aegean University in Greece, 68
alternative path, 96
alternative resource, 94, 96
alternative teaching approaches, 8
American and Latvian systems, 83
American and Ukrainian cultures, 84, 93
American and Ukrainian economic systems, 77
American and Ukrainian educational systems and economic systems, 124
American education system, 47
American, Greek, Latvian and Ukrainian academic systems, 45
American, Latvian, Polish, Ukrainian, and Hungarian academic systems, 46
amiable communication, 98
amiable teaching and learning atmosphere, 127
analogies and contrasts between different cultures, 123
analytical skills and comparisons, 17
applications of difference equations in robotics, 52
asking questions versus answering questions, 125
asking the right questions, 10, 13, 51, 90, 92–93, 123
asynchronous style, 134
available resources, 56, 88, 90

B

background and preparation levels, 22
balance between leading and following, 125
bases of knowledge, 62
bridging them together, 110
building international collaborations, 49

C

co-ops, 13
collaboration, 12, 77
collaborative learning, 80
colleagues' feedback, 10

147

colleagues' suggestions, 99
combinations of math disciplines, 63
common mistakes, 125
communication skills, 62, 76, 131
compare similarities and differences, 77
comparing analogies, 108, 110
comparing educational systems, 49
comparing similarities and differences between concepts, 127
composition and design, 79
concepts, 106
concrete representation, 30
constructive criticisms, 99
contrasts between the American and Ukrainian economic systems, 110
course evaluations, 38
creative solutions, 125
critical thinking skills, 62, 76, 89, 101, 131
cross-cultural comparisons, 5, 10, 114, 123
cross-cultural experiences, 135
cultural balance, 23
cultural barriers, 5
cultural changes, 27
cultural influence, 11–12
cultures, 106, 110

D

decipher cross-cultural comparisons, 77
deeper interpretations, 62
design and promotion of new seminars and courses, 52
designing your story, 112
detecting contrasts, 110
detecting missing themes, 113
developing innovations, 108, 110
developing international & interdisciplinary research coalitions, 6, 18, 52, 56–57, 80, 83, 85, 91, 94, 96, 123, 130
development of new techniques, 62

difference between good questions and right questions, 123
different academic system and culture, 22
different culture, 21
different educational system, 21
disciplines, 106
discrete mathematics, 66
distance courses, 117
distance education, 118
distance learning programs, 117–118
dynamic teaching and learning atmosphere, 123

E

economic influence, 13
economic systems, 84
educational reforms, 9
educational systems, 20–21, 110
effective communication, 15, 19, 131
effective communication skills, 118
efficiency and multitasking, 127
efficient communication, 131
EKA University of Applied Sciences in Riga, Latvia, 46, 82
electronic white board, 127, 135
emotional intelligence, 8
essential characteristics of feedback, 98
establishing international & interdisciplinary research coalitions, 113
exceeding the expected outcomes, 115
exchange of ideas, 18
expand your horizons, 113
expanding international horizons, 49
expansion of international and multidisciplinary horizons, 129
expansion of international education, 20
expansion of international horizons, 20, 41
expansion of the digital era, 118
expected learning outcomes and beyond, 119–120, 122–125

experiences and intuitions, 29, 62, 76, 93, 131
experiential learning, 9
extensions and multiple re-submissions, 33
extensions on homework assignments, 122, 125

F

face-to-face conferences, 131
face-to-face environment, 136
fast and instant exchange of information, 126
feedback from colleagues and friends, 38, 89, 96–99
flexibility to feedback, 15, 89, 96, 99, 113, 125
flexibility to students' feedback, 28, 38
flexible and open to feedback, 113
flexible teaching and learning environment, 13
fundamental attributes of developing innovations, 108
future improvements and innovations, 45

G

globalization, 22
Google Meets, 134

H

hand-on teaching and learning atmosphere, 13
hands-on courses and seminars, 22, 79, 85
hands-on multidisciplinary course, 78, 83
hands-on multidisciplinary seminar, 80
hands-on practice problems, 38, 90
hands-on projects, 12
hands-on teaching and learning environment, 7

hands-on teaching and learning style, 28–29, 67
hands-on teaching tactic, 29, 31
holistic approach, 18
horizons, 76
hybrid environment, 120

I

innovation, 7, 19
instant graded feedback, 129
international and multidisciplinary collaborations, 131
international and multidisciplinary conferences, 21
international and multidisciplinary education, 13
international and multidisciplinary horizons, 94
international and multidisciplinary level, 19
international and multidisciplinary research coalitions, 94
international and multidisciplinary research projects, 80
international association advanced distributed learning, 118
international atmosphere, 129
international collaborations and innovations, 20, 49
international conferences, 80
international education and collaborations, 16, 41
international experiences, 80
international face-to-face environment, 137
international horizons, 41
international influence, 12, 27
international Math Olympiad, 70
international pedagogy, 21, 59
international relations, 41
International Scientific Symposium "Economics, Business & Finance", in Jurmala, Latvia, 51
introducing new ideas and practices, 45

introduction recognition & deciphering of patterns, 108, 110
introduction to business start-ups, 46, 55, 57, 77, 83, 85, 91, 93, 96, 101, 110, 113–114, 124, 129
introduction to complex variables, 129
introduction to difference equations, 67
Introduction to Math Olympiad, 46, 52, 55
Introduction to Math Olympics, 71, 101
Introduction to Olympiad Problems, 71
Introduction to Photography Course, 78, 85, 90
Introduction to Recognition & Deciphering of Patterns, 4, 21, 30, 51–52, 55, 57, 62, 68, 90, 94, 115, 124
intuitions, 62, 76, 131
investigate new research questions, 127

J

Jeans, Blue, 134
journey to new discoveries, 21

L

limited resources, 58, 100–102

M

Math Olympics in American Style Event, 6, 46, 70–71, 90, 113
MATHBOWL, 48, 70–71, 90
mathematical horizons, 61–63
maximizing the outcomes, 102
Microsoft Teams, 134
more opportunities to ask detailed questions, 128
more participants ask questions during online conferences, 131
multi-step and multi-task problems, 63

multidisciplinary and international horizons, 5, 78
multidisciplinary education, 16–18
multidisciplinary hands-on course, 85
multidisciplinary hands-on seminar, 85
multidisciplinary horizons and collaborations, 75, 77–78, 84
multidisciplinary influence, 12
multiple colors, 28
multiple files at the same time, 127
multiple questions and comments, 127
multiple re-submissions of homework assignments, 28, 122, 125

N

natural sources, 21
new academic innovations, 21
new academic system, 54
new courses and seminars, 22
new doors and windows of perspectives, 45
new ideas, 98–99
new improvements, 38
new innovations and discoveries, 18, 38, 94
new innovative directions, 77
new international and multidisciplinary relations, 92
new international and multidisciplinary research collaborations, 130
new international frontiers emerge, 76, 133, 135
new international horizons, 135
new learning skills, 127
new perspectives, 55
new practices, 99
new research collaborations, 130
new research directions, 130, 131
new research methods and directions, 98
new teaching innovations, 13, 21, 118
new teaching practices, 131

new teaching techniques and practices, 98
new windows and doors of opportunities, 133
non-standard and non-traditional solutions, 94
non-standard approach to solving a specific problem, 89
non-standard approaches, 90
non-standard solutions, 123
non-standard thinking, 18
notice specific details and problems, 93–94

O

old teaching methods, 9
online atmosphere, 124
online conferences welcome more international participants, 130–131
online courses, 38, 127–129, 135
online courses synchronously, 98
online education, 117, 119–120
online environment, 83, 127, 133, 135–136
online lectures, 135
online meetings, conferences, 134
online seminars, 136
online teaching and learning atmosphere, 83–84, 119, 129
online teaching and learning practice, 134
online teaching, learning and working environment, 118, 120, 131, 134–136

P

pedagogical innovations, 7–8
Periodic & Eventually Periodic Solutions of Max-Type and Piecewise Difference Equations, 52
positive learning atmosphere, 13
positive teaching and learning atmosphere, 13

practical experiences, 9
practice problems, 122
practices, 30, 118
presenting a welcoming story, 124
primary and secondary resources, 89
primary resources, 88–90
principles of photography, 79
problem solving skills and competitive skills, 62, 76, 131
problem solving techniques, 76
problem solving tool, 7
professional and new potential collaboration opportunities, 130
prompt feedback, 28, 128

R

recognition and deciphering of patterns, 68
repetition, 31
repetitive-style practice problems, 30–31
repetitive-style problems, 28
repetitive-type guided examples, 122
repetitive-type practice problems, 12, 64, 94
revising your innovation, 113
Rezekne Technical Academy High School, 68
Riga Technical University Department of Engineering Economics & Management recommended, 46, 51, 78, 82, 96
Riga Technical University Doctoral School, 81, 91
Risk Management Seminar, 10, 52, 58, 78, 82–83, 85, 96, 113, 130
Rochester Institute of Technology, 45

S

SAT preparatory course, 4, 6, 55, 65–66, 71, 115

Scholastic Aptitude Test (SAT), 47
secondary resources address, 88–91
selling your idea, 114
similarities and differences between academic systems, 45
similarities and differences between educational systems, 41
similarities between concepts, disciplines and cultures, 108
Skype, 134
Society, Integration, Education International Scientific Conference in Rezekne, 51
solve more challenging problems, 129
solving problems, 8, 114–115
students' evaluations, 81
students' feedback, 10, 15, 38
students' intuition, 22
students' learning styles, 8, 11, 21–22
students' performance, 27
students' preparation levels and their learning styles, 8, 5, 21, 23, 57
students' value orientations, 21, 57
successful leadership, 98
successful mathematics teaching tactics, 120
successful outcomes, 89
successful teaching practices, 120
suggesting ideas versus listening to ideas, 125
swift and efficient communication, 131
swift exchange of information, 131
swift graded feedback, 127
synchronous style of online communication, 134
system of diminishing equilateral triangles, 108–109
system of equilateral triangles, 111
system of shrinking squares, 108
system of squares, 111

T

teaching principles, 54
teaching style and learning style, 23
teaching versus learning, 125
technological advances, 27
technology influence, 11
thinking outside and beyond your comfort zone, 17
thinking outside your box, 17
thinking outside your comfort zone, 18, 90, 93–94
time of the year, 57
traditional face-to-face and in online environments, 120
traditional face-to-face conferences, 131
traditional face-to-face environment, 134, 136
traditional face-to-face local and regional conferences, 130
traditional face-to-face teaching and learning environment, 123
Transportation & Sakaru Institute, 66, 68
trust level, 15

U

UNESCO, 118
unfold new discoveries and challenges, 123
unique selling traits, 79, 106
University of Latvia, 70
unlike patterns, 121
unlimited access to notes and videos, 128
use of multiple colors, 34

V

value orientations, 8–9
video platforms, 127

W

weekly homework assignments, 84
workshop-based Calculus at RIT, 63, 66
writing a welcoming story, 114–115
written comments, 14

Y

Yuriy Bugay International & Scientific Technical University, 113

Z

Zoom, 126, 134

www.ingramcontent.com/pod-product-compliance
Lightning Source LLC
Chambersburg PA
CBHW070309230426
43664CB00015B/2700